Book Reviews and Testimonials

Reading Mike's book, Alive and Thrivin', makes me want to take up a hobby. Preferably something other than reading. Gary Moore, Mike's Favorite Real Estate Client.

I hope the success of this book, Alive and Thrivin', will allow Mike to finally break down and hire a landscape maintenance crew. His yard is atrocious. Mike Bingham, Mike's neighbor.

Mike Copeland, is a rascal and a scalawag. You're never quite sure what kind of shenanigans he's up as a writer – Steve Fuller, Mike's Retirement Counselor.

Alive and Thrivin' is a titillating read. I'm only kidding. I just like saying the word titillating. Jason Allen, Mike's real estate protégé.

First book – no horse, second book – no horse. Third book, forget the horse, I want a new car. How about a Mustang? See what I did there? Hannah Copeland, Mike's Eldest Daughter.

I'm not even going to ask what this book is about because I didn't get the appeal of the first two books. Claire Copeland, Mike's Youngest Daughter.

When it comes to writing, Michael is a real mensch. It's Yiddish, look it up. Ellen Warshaw, Mike's Mother-in-law.

I thought Alive and Thrivin' was a story about Kaiser Permanente and how difficult it is to stay alive with when you have Kaiser Permanente as your medical provider. Dave Jones, Mike's Business Networking Consultant.

Mike is an extremely charitable person, giving both his time and money to community causes. After reading his book, Alive and Thriving, I'm sure he'll be giving these away as well. Kathy Chiverton, Discovery Counseling Center

I pray for Mike and his writing. Tyler Scott, Senior Pastor at Community Presbyterian Church (#forthevalley).

Mike, who became a humorist, and myself, who became a comic, both played football for Cal State Northridge. The only college sports program that recruited Mark Twain and Dick Van Dyke prototypes. Horrible teams, but great parties. READ THIS BOOK! Bryan Kellen, Mike's Favorite Stand-up Comedian.

Congratulations dummy, you just bought a book of essays that were previously printed in a free magazine. Tony Camin, Mike's Favorite Stand-up Comedian.

We shouldn't have sacrificed so many trees for the printing of these awful books. Scott Ellis, Mike's primary commercial real estate rival.

alive & thrivin'

alive & thrivin'

Michael S. Copeland

ABOOKS

ALIVE and Thrivin'
Copyright © 2020 by Michael S. Copeland

All rights reserved.
No part of this book may be reproduced or transmitted in any form or by any means without written permission from the publisher and author.

Additional copies may be ordered from the publisher for educational, business, promotional or premium use.
For information, contact ALIVE Book Publishing at: alivebookpublishing.com, or call (925) 837-7303.

Book Design by Alex Johnson

ISBN 13
978-1-63132-089-7

Library of Congress Control Number: 2020903776

Library of Congress Cataloging-in-Publication Data is available upon request.

First Edition

Published in the United States of America by
ALIVE Book Publishing and ALIVE Publishing Group, imprints of Advanced Publishing LLC
3200 A Danville Blvd., Suite 204, Alamo, California 94507
alivebookpublishing.com

PRINTED IN THE UNITED STATES OF AMERICA

10 9 8 7 6 5 4 3 2 1

DEDICATION

To me, religion and spirituality are deeply personal beliefs, that's why it might surprise many to know that this book is dedicated to GOD. To say that I've been blessed is an understatement. I am so incredibly grateful for the wonderful life I've lived, for the loving and supportive family and friends that I have, and for all of the good times I've experienced. Whatever the future holds, I know God is by my side.

TABLE OF CONTENTS

Foreword By Hannah Copeland   13
Foreword By Claire Copeland   15
Acknowledgements   17

I. Live and Let Live   19

1. I'm Not Old, Just Older   21
2. Spring Break, A Break We All Need   25
3. The Spring Clean   29
4. Spring has Sprung   33
5. Beware of Hotel Hell   37
6. Comedy is Serious Business   41
7. Summer Writer's Block – Block Party   47
8. Summer Writer's Block Vol. 2   51
9. Summer Writer's Block Vol. 3   55
10. Summer Writer's Block Vol. 4   61
11. Summer Writer's Block Vol. 5   67
12. It's My Birthday   73
13. Mika's Houseboat Ark   79
14. Everyone Has a Book in Them   83
15. It's a Dog's Life   89
16. It's Tough to be a Kid   93
17. Dan Donnelly – Tailgate Entrepreneur   99
18. My Beer Garden   103
19. Our International Pub Crawl   107
20. I am the Last Emperor   113
21. The Rain in Spain   117

22. Time Traveling for Summer Vacation	123
23. Whatever Happened to Custom Service – Part II	129
24. Where Does the Time Go?	133
25. What's It Like to Be…….	137
26. You're Not a Millennial if……	143

II. Dad Speak   147

1. My Little Girls are Growing Up Too Fast	149
2. I'm Not as Frugal as My Father	153
3. The Prospective College Road Show	157
4. High School Graduation Day	161
5. Making a Difference by Volunteering	165
6. Dadisms	169
7. College Kids and Parents Weekend	175
8. Savor the Moments	179

III. Holiday Madness   183

1. Finding the Holiday Spirit	185
2. A Thanksgiving Day Story	189
3. Pass Me the Drumstick	193
4. They Call Me Mr. Claus	197
5. The White Elephant Gift Exchange	201
6. My Star Wars New Year	205
7. One Writer's Voice	209
8. The Valentine's Day Advice Column	213
9. I'm A Yankee Doodle Dandy	217
10. Preserving the Magic Words	221
11. An Astrological New Year	225
12. Halloweek	229
13. If I lived at the North Pole	233
14. Thanksgiving Carols	237

IV. My Music and Musical Friends   241

1. Paul Jefferson – Nashville Singer Songwriter   243
2. David Victor – Rock Stars & Stripes   249
3. Suzanna Spring – Blending Music and Yoga   255
4. John Floyd Killen – Cover Band King   259
5. The Music in me   263
6. My Concert/Comedy History   267
7. The Lasting Appeal of Boybands   275

FOREWORD
BY HANNAH COPELAND

It is difficult to sum up my dad in only a few words, let alone three paragraphs. My earliest memories of my dad stem back to when I was in kindergarten and on Wednesdays he would drive me to school. On that day, I would sit in his bathroom and watch him shave while he got ready for work. I loved the methodical way he tied his tie, the smell of his cologne and the banter between 5 year old me and adult him. It was one of the times I cherish the most with him. Wednesdays were my favorite day of the week because I got that special one-on-one time with him, but it was also my least favorite day because I hated saying goodbye when it was time for him to go to work. My dad is my protector, my hero, my shoulder to cry on, and the person I aspire to be the most like. He has taught me kindness, patience, confidence and many other "life lessons" as he calls them. He often tells me that life lessons are hardly ever painless or inexpensive, but an important part of growing up. Whenever I find myself in some kind of trouble, he is always there to rescue me. I know I can go to him for anything and even if he and I hit a rough patch, he is there to tell me, "Even when I'm mad at you, I still love you". I can only hope that one day I can have the same patience for my children that my dad has for me, and to teach them the same essential life lessons.

I've watched my dad perform random acts of kindness time after time for countless people. He would bring in my elderly neighbor's newspaper to her front door every day, he would wash someone's car or mow their lawn "just because". He often would leave bags of used clothes and shoes for the homeless in San Francisco. His kindness is infectious and I can't help but smile when I see him doing volunteer or community service work and think, "That's my dad". Most people go through their day so focused on the stress and problems in their own life that they ignore everyone else along the way. My dad can see beyond his own world and know that by doing one little act, it can make someone else's day so much better. He showed me how kindness can not only change other's lives, but your own life as well. He's taught me how to forgive and how far it goes to just simply say "I'm sorry" sometimes.

Not many men can measure up to the man my dad is, nor can they compare to the father he is. He has been the greatest role model, cheerleader, and knight in shining armor to me and my sister. I don't tell him often enough how incredibly proud I am of him and all that he has accomplished (writing three books, running a marathon, performing stand-up comedy), and all that he will accomplish (walking his daughters down the aisle, becoming a grandpa and enjoying retirement...hopefully soon). I often joke that my dad should become the mayor of Danville, because everyone knows him and no one has anything bad to say about him. Honestly, it's true. He is a selfless man and puts himself before others. As a coach, he has encouraged the boys on his Thunderbird football teams to be confident young men and as an umpire with SRVGAL, he empowers the girls to be strong and resilient. I have never minded sharing him with others because I know just how fortunate I am to have a dad like my dad.

FOREWORD
BY CLAIRE COPELAND

At times, I wonder who benefits the most from my dad's articles. Is it friends, family, people in the dentist office waiting room who have nothing to look at, but there just so conveniently happens to be an ALIVE magazine (because my dad had personally put them there himself) or is it me? Without his creative, passionate, humor filled assistance many of my school papers would be pretty boring and bad. Ever since my dad started writing articles, I can tell he's doing something he really loves. My dad is naturally a funny guy who has a lot to say and writing articles could not have been a better fit for him. When I was younger, I didn't like writing very much, but watching him craft something new every month for ALIVE inspired to appreciate writing much more. Writing is a way to show who you are and express your thoughts.

My dad and I are very much alike in many ways. For starters, we have the same sarcastic, self-deprecating sense of humor. I find it very rewarding being able to put a smile on someone's face and make them laugh by saying or writing something humorous. That's a gift I got from my dad. Thanks to my dad, I have also learned to appreciate and enjoy the little things and precious moments in life and to perform random acts of kindness.

One of my favorite things about my dad writing these articles, is finding ALIVE magazines in hidden places. They might be in the side panel of my car, stuffed in my suitcase or backpack, next to the toilet of my apartment or dorm bathroom at school and they even manage to show up at my friend's houses. They seem to follow me everywhere. When my dad wants me to do something he often says, "It will only take two minutes" and reading his articles really does only take 2 minutes. I find myself smiling and laughing with each vignette in large part because I can hear his voice as I read. I especially enjoy reading them when there's distance between us.

Without his articles I wouldn't be able to brag to my friends that my dad writes for a magazine, has two books in publication and that I got to meet Captain Sully Sullenberger (my dad interviewed him for a profile piece). I can really tell how much each article means to him and it inspires me to find something I'm really passionate about in my life. My dad has taught me so much in life and I'll be forever grateful. I'm so happy for him competing his third book. What an accomplishment. Love you!

ACKNOWLEDGEMENTS

I always knew that once I wrote my first book there would be three books in the trilogy, because that's what a trilogy is, a group of three dramatic or literary works related in subject or theme. Think about all the successful book trilogies that have been written over the years including *The Hunger Games, Divergent, Girl with the Dragon Tattoo* and even *50 Shades of Grey*. I think more of the classic novels should have been trilogies. I bet Truman Capote wishes he had thought of a trilogy when he penned *In Cold Blood*. There could have been an *In Cold Blood Part Deux* and *Part III* or *In Cold Plasma* and *In Cold Hemoglobin*.

One of my daughter Hannah's favorite novel series was *Twilight* which was originally just a trilogy until the author, Stephanie Meyer decided to get greedy and write a fourth book about vampire lust and werewolf gangs. The incredibly creative J.K. Rowling was so inspired by boy wizard *Harry Potter* and his friends that she churned out two trilogies plus one. I don't have that much patience or energy. I'm pretty confident, now that my third book has been released, it, like the prestigious list above will almost assuredly secure a movie deal. I hope Bruce Willis plays me.

I have always thanked my family first and foremost. Julie, Hannah & Claire have provided a deep well of love, inspiration and support for all my writing projects, especially the columns and books. Thank you. I have a special, and at times dysfunctional, connection and appreciation for my sisters; Christine, Cathy and Mitzi who I'm very grateful are in my corner. Finally, my cousin Ben is a man I have always looked up to and admired for his levity, strength of character and good heart.

I would like to thank my risk management and quality control team that includes Vanisha Kumar, Stan Wilson, Jennifer Burton, Mike Mooney, Jim Fairchild, Peggy Warshaw, Dave Stallard, Erin Downey, Felicia Faravelli-Soares and Kathy Chiverton, Zack Haller, Mark Heavey and Kurt Chambliss.

Finally, I would like to thank my network of guy friends, one female friend and a few kids, whose wit and sarcasm provide the creative mental workouts I require to come up with my monthly humor lifestyle pieces for ALIVE magazine. Thanks to Burt Harris, Jason Allen, Gary Moore, Gayle Thomas, John Floyd Killen, Matt Cheeseman, Blake Chauvin, Jason Chandler and Robert Price, along with his children (Sarina, Logan, Juliette and Hudson).

My humor lifestyle writing idol, hero and unauthorized mentor, is Dave Berry. Mr. Berry has over 25 books out on a variety of topics such as parenting, aging, traveling, the holidays, home repair, health and fitness, money management, etc. In roughly 1985, I read one of Mr. Berry's weekly columns in the San Jose Mercury News and I was hooked. His humor and wit inspired me to work on my craft and feel proud enough about the material I was writing to submit it to editors, like Eric "Chief" Johnson at ALIVE. The fact that Eric liked my material was recognition enough, however knowing that he and I have worked together for over 13 years is icing on the cake. He is truly a friend, motivator and wonderful boss. To be able to say that I am a monthly columnist in a popular regional magazine is beyond my wildest dreams.

If you're reading the Acknowledgements in a self-published book, which is essentially a compilation of magazine articles you, are either very close to me, you were given this book as a gift from me or you're being tortured by our government. Regardless, thank you and I hope you enjoy what I have to offer.

I
Live and Let Live

One of my mantras in life is "live and let live." My friends, family, co-workers and acquaintances would all likely, probably, hopefully say that I am a lot of things, but a hypocrite is not one of them. In my columns, I do my best to make humorous observations about issues and events, times, trials and tribulations. Who am I kidding? I enjoy using a self-deprecating form of levity to make light of trivial or heavy topics. Simply put, I like to poke fun at stuff.

I credit my childhood friends Derek Sousa and Jeff Morales for laying the ground work for these types of observations. We started writing humor lifestyle pieces before we had any readers or the form even had a genre. I also credit people like David Vanavermaete, Stan Wilson, Rob Price, Julie Copeland, Ben Seeker, my daughters Hannah and Claire, and the woman at the dental office of Melanie Koehler, D.D.S with helping me not only to find humor in everyday subject matter, but also challenging me to bring my "A" game when it comes to wit and humor. Our conversations, texts and emails were the kindling for many of my finest fiery columns.

I'm Not Old, Just older

Like the eternally youthful Jon Bon Jovi sings in his song "Just Older," "I like the bed I'm sleeping in, it's just like me it's broken in/It's not old, just older. Like a favorite pair of torn blue jeans, this skin I'm in it's alright with me! It's not old, just older." When that song came out in the year 2000, Jon was thirty-eight years old. That's not old at all. Today, John and I are roughly the same age, pushing fifty-four and we're definitely getting older. However, he's probably aged a little better thanks to a massive collection of thirty-year-old rock star groupies. My magazine groupies tend to be sixty-five-year old shut-ins with lots of cats.

Rationally, I know that I'm older, but most days I don't really feel that much older than I did ten or twenty years ago. Sure, some days getting out of bed is a bit more challenging than it used to be, but overall I believe age is more a state of mind. My energy level is still strong, and I'm vibrant and viral. I'm up on popular music (Fetty Wap, Hozier and the Bieb), I like the current cast of SNL (Aidy Bryant, Taran Killam, Leslie Jones, Pete Davidson and Cecily Strong) and I can even name every player on the Golden State Warriors (including James Michael McAdoo, Festus Ezeli and Mo Buckets). Most nights I can stay awake until almost 11:30 pm, (later if I have get a nap during the day or drink an afternoon Red Bull), I still mow my own lawn and I regularly log 10,000 daily steps on my FitBit. It's probably safe to say that most men in their forties aspire to be in my type of physical and mental youthful state of mind and body.

In April of 2011, I wrote an article entitled "I Might Be a Dinosaur." Being forty-nine years old at the time, I was fearful that my friends and I were headed for extinction because we were showing signs of sluggishness, contentment, being slow to adapt and resistant of change. Since that time, I think I've stepped up my game. I've lost a little weight, updated my wardrobe at Forever 51 and I've been watching *American Horror Story* on the FX network despite the fact that I find it very disturbing. I might never be confused for a Millennial, but I wouldn't necessarily want to be a snobby tech-centric, SOMO living, hoverboard burning, Lyft riding, skinny pants wearing, app loving thirty-birdy.

If I were old, which I'm not, I would know that I was old if I started to recognize the following signs:

If you complain of being sore the day after an evening bocce ball match, you might be getting old.

If you complain that your kid's music is too loud.... when they're wearing headphones, you might be getting old.

If you fall asleep at the dinner table during a "late" meal and it's only 7:30, you might be getting old.

If your idea of walking the dog is to the front door and back, you might be getting old.

If your kids regularly ask you if you went to school with Abraham Lincoln, Amelia Earhart, Babe Ruth or Jesus, you might be getting old.

If you color your hair because the drapes don't match the carpet anymore, you might be getting old.

If you avoid activities such as bowling, dancing and yard work because you can't risk the chance of injury, you might be getting old.

If your kids believe their parents might have been abducted by aliens and they're now being raised by their grandparents, you might be getting old.

If your wife bought you a piece of jewelry for Valentine's Day with the inscription DNR, you might be getting old.

If you only shop at stores that have a section of sensible shoes, you might be getting old.

If your idea of "going commando" includes adult diapers, you might be getting old.

If you need a nap before you have lunch on the weekend, you might be getting old.

If you enjoy getting the monthly AARP magazine for the articles and discount coupons, you might be getting old.

If most of your conversations begin with the term, "Back in my day", you might be getting old.

If the last song you "downloaded" was buying the cassette version of "I Can't Fight This Feeling" by REO Speedwagon, you might be getting old.

If your idea of "going green" means more kale in your diet, you might be getting old.

If you can really relate to my monthly humor lifestyle articles in *ALIVE*, you might be getting old.

When I was in my teens, I thought anyone over forty was old.

When I was in my thirties, anyone in their fifties seemed old. Now that I'm in my fifties, seventy really doesn't sound so old. I heard somewhere that as we age we begin to lose our hearing, sight and memory. At least I think that's what someone said; I don't really remember because I couldn't hear or see that person very well. I'm not old, just older, just like a few of my childhood idols who still rock with a boat load of swag. Anyone ever heard of Sir Paul McCartney, age 73, Dan Rather, age 84, Pete Rose, age 74, Hugh Heffner, age 89, Mean Joe Greene, age 69, Al Pacino, age 74, and Astronaut Buzz Aldrin, 85?

My dog Trudy is old. She's twelve in people years, which is 84 in dog years. She sleeps a lot and moves slowly. She complains about her aches and pains (with grunts) and is often gassy. She is picky about what she eats and she goes outside about forty times a day to "do her business." Up until I wrote the part about going outside, I could have been describing my mother-in-law.

When I am old, I'll look forward to taking care of my yard, playing golf with my buddies and cheering on our local sports teams. In other words, pretty much doing what I do now on any given weekend. My actual plan includes playing with my future grandchildren, traveling the world and taking advantage of the early bird special at Applebee's. I don't fear getting old, I'm just not in any hurry to get there. There's too much to do leading up to the time when I can't do it, whatever "it" happens to be. Until then, I'm not old/just getting older, day by day.

2 Spring Break
A break we all need

Spring break is just the break I need to break from the monotonous routine I find myself in this time of year. Like many of my readers, both of you, I get up (when it's still dark outside), make school lunches, eat breakfast, see the kids off, drive to work, put in an exhausting day at the salt mines, drive home (in the dark), eat dinner, read a little, watch some TV and go to bed. Fear not, this isn't a "woe is me" article, although it could be if I added the stuff about bill paying, dog walking and helping with homework. I know spring break was designed to give students a one-week break from their studies, but believe me when I say, spring break can't come soon enough for this suburban superhero.

In years past, my family and I have gone to Lake Tahoe, Washington D.C., New York City, and we even did a Caribbean cruise with the in-laws one year. One more day on a ship with my mother-in-law and I would have been dangerously close to jumping overboard. It really doesn't matter where what your ultimate destination is as long as we get out of Dodge for a week. We don't actually live in Dodge, but you get my drift. Marshall Dillon and Miss Kitty once lived in Dodge on the long-running western, *Gunsmoke*. I wonder if they actually "got out of Dodge" during spring break. You have to admit, "Get out of Dodge" sounds a lot better than "Get out of Danville." Danville is where Phineas and Ferb live. Phineas and Ferb is a delightful Disney Channel series. I know that because my sad routine includes occasionally watching cartoons. I bet even Phineas and Ferb want to get out of Danville for spring break.

I'm not complaining, I'm commiserating. Who's with me? We don't actually have to go on our spring break vacation together, unless you want to, but metaphorically speaking, aren't we all ready for a spring break? A break from our lives., our jobs, our commitments is a good thing.. It can recharge the battery, stoke the fire or just save your sanity.

Where are you planning to go for spring break this year?

Hawaii. Who doesn't love Hawaii? —Monica C.

A college road trip with my high school son. Utah, Colorado, New Mexico, Arizona. —Scott W.

Disneyland. It's the happiest place on earth. —Cindy G.

Skiing in Tahoe. If there's enough snow. Is there enough snow? —Jason A.

Huntington Beach. Sun and fun. —George P.

We're doing a San Francisco "staycation." We'll be sightseeing like European tourists. —Mike B.

We wanted to go to spring training in Arizona, but spring break is late this year so we're heading to San Diego to see the Padres play baseball and go to the zoo. —Alexis P.

Those destinations all sound very tame and nice, but certainly nothing like the spring breaks of our college day. Spring break originally gained notoriety sometime in the early 80's with the hedonistic college pilgrimage to the legendary Fort Lauderdale. Subsequently, new haunts such as Daytona Beach, South Padre Island, Palm Springs and Las Vegas started drawing the post-high-school collegiate crowd. I don't want to brag (yes I do), but I tore it up pretty good back in the day in places such as Lake

Havasu, San Diego and Palm Desert. It wasn't a *Girls Gone Wild* video (on one occasion it was), but a few of those SBs were epic.

In College, where was your best spring break spent?

An RV trip to Palm Springs. We trashed the RV and lost our deposit, but it was worth it. —Mark D.

Miami Beach. Sun, clubs and the beach. It was a blast. —Rhonda N.

There was a wild trip to Lake Tahoe in '94, but the terms of my probation prohibit me from talking about it. —Justin G.

Probably New Orleans, but I don't remember a lot of it. —Blake C.

Skiing in Taos, New Mexico. Life was good back then. —Tyler B.

Mazatlan, Mexico. I got shaken down by the local police and had to buy my way out of trouble. It was sketchy, but it makes for a great story. —Matt M.

Camping in Yosemite with my college girlfriend was the best spring break I ever spent. I still think about it. Don't tell my wife. —Joe D. (not his real name).

There may have been a time in my younger days when a swim suit, wet suit or my birthday suit were the body surfing/bonfire party apparel options of a wild time at pick-a-name beach somewhere along the California coast. I was the king of the Beer- Bong, the Body Shot and the Ice Breaker. Now, if my teen daughters ask what those vile terms mean, I tell them they're games invented by the devil and most assuredly cause cancer. It would be an interesting case study to dissect what we recklessly enjoyed as young adults and how we don't want our senveteen-to-twenty-two-year-olds to experience any of it. As the head of our family, my job is to show the kids a part of the country and cherish the quality time I get to spend with my girls. With college looming, I fear that they'll be exposed to spring break boys, the type their dad used to be like, all too soon.

Maybe this year we'll just throw all our stuff in the car and head to places unknown without a preset destination. Yea, like that could ever happen. We're all about the preparation, anticipation and the execution of the spring break. We're a "tion" family. Granted, the theme and destination of my spring breaks may have been altered since the craziness of my youth, but they are still an important staple in my life. It's a break we all need right now.

3 Spring Clean
The House, Yard and Garage Beautification

Spring is in the air. Birds are chirping, flowers are blooming and the Giants are at Spring Training in Arizona. Now that we've all given up on our New Year's resolutions, or at least postponed them until after Easter, it's time to think about spring cleaning. That traditional time of year when we plan a major clean-up of our house, yard and the garage. This is no easy chore (or collection of chores). It takes preparation, conditioning and training. Back when I was a kid, my parents took great pleasure in participating in our annual springtime neighborhood beautification project. I can still remember my mother's spring cleaning slogan of 1973, "Clean it and I mean it" or her 1979 catch phrase, "If it don't fit, it ain't legit," which I'm pretty sure was stolen by Johnny Cochran for his OJ defense years later. My all-time favorite was 1985's "My louse of a spouse better clean this damn house." I think my mom was mad at my dad that year. In most households, spring cleaning still remains a necessary evil and the month of March is when most families begin to tackle this ritualistic effort.

The House. These days, when everyone needs the newest, fastest and coolest of everything, where nothing is built to last but everything is recyclable, a lot of us accumulate an excessive amount of junk around the house. Growing up, my parents insisted that during SC week, we would pack up our home like we were moving across country. This fun little task allowed us to throw out, clean up and organize the contents of our 1,800-square foot house after 11.75 months of hoarding, storing and ignoring the place. It was amazing what we would find around the house as we emptied out closets, rearranged furniture and unloaded cabinets and cupboards. Sadly, anything from a Santa suit to old Halloween candy to a petrified missing pet could potentially be uncovered. Discoveries like would inevitably bring up a few interesting questions, such as . . . why did Santa leave his suit at our house, who's the chocoholic hoarding Kit Kat bars and why did the hamster commit suicide? Room by room, the Copeland Clan would ascend on our targeted living space assignment with one goal: to beautificate the premises.

As parents, the term *clean up* may be too simplistic a term when it comes to the thought of tackling the hard hat excavation of our kid's bedrooms and closets. I am always amazed at the amount of "stuff" kids of today can accumulate. My daughters' rooms often resemble a stinky secondhand thrift store? I like to think of spring cleaning the kid's bedrooms as the great discard of accumulated worthless junk, a purging of broken and obsolete electronics and the general discarding of non-fitting or out-of-style clothing. If memory serves me correctly, I didn't have one tenth of the stuff my kids have lying around the house. I owned one pair of sneakers, not what seems like hundreds of running shoes, flip-flops, boots, slippers, flats and heels. Not that I wanted a pair of heels. I wasn't a young Bruce Jenner.

The Yard. My landscape isn't in any better shape than the house. Despite a lack of rain, I have weeds in my lawn, weeds in my shrubs, weeds in my rock beds and weeds in the cracks of my concrete/driveway. Even my beautifully stone BBQ island has weeds. Not to mention, every plantlike green thing outside of my house is overgrown to the point that my backyard looks like the Amazon rainforest or a Rainforest Café. Back in the day, my Dad would rally his pre-pubescent children around him on a Saturday morning and begin by having us spray the yard with the strongest pre and post emergent chemicals sold (illegally) at black market flea markets. Once that was complete, he would give us access to the sharpest machete type gardening tools in the shed for a hardy afternoon of pruning, trimming and weeding. Finally, after a refreshing ten-minute lunch break, he would point us in the direction of the riding mower. But hey, except for an occasional tick or tremor, I turned out OK. Now those pesky OSHA restrictions and child labor laws limit our kids to raking leaves and using the hose. I can't even get the little buggers to clean up the dog poop. If it weren't against the HOA CC&Rs, this would be the perfect time of year to shape my agapanthus shrubs into the shape of various zoo animals. Truth be told, my yard just needs some mulch, a few flowers and a synthetic lawn to keep my neighbors from shaking their heads in disgust as they drive by the house and refuse to wave.

The Garage. The garage is the biggest and most difficult of the three Spring Cleaning Triathlon events. It will take strength, endurance and steroids (use them if you've got them) to get the wife's car back into its rightful spot. It is not uncommon to fill every square inch of my garage each year, much like a hoarder's self-storage unit in Richmond. Last spring, I found my next-door neighbor's ping-pong table, kegerator and his mother-in-law living in my garage. I have no idea how any of those things got there, but I did return his ping-pong table.

A proper garage spring cleaning can consume an entire weekend. First thing Saturday morning, l slip into my Haz-mat suit and Chuck Taylor high tops and begin removing every last item from the garage and placing it in alphabetical order on the front lawn and driveway. Just kidding, I just throw shi..stuff anywhere. Once the garage is swept, power washed and de-loused, there's the job of storing everything to an orderly place, less the 70% of previous inventory that gets trashed, hauled, donated or sold at Sunday's big Copeland Family White Trash Garage Sale. There will be price-slashing specials all day long. If all goes we'll, I can usually park the little woman's car back in the garage for about a week or two before we start accumulating new junk and the garage becomes overrun again.

It's been said that our home is our castle! Spring-cleaning is a great opportunity to spruce up the kingdom. For most of us, our house is our single largest investment and a little curb appeal wouldn't hurt the value. There's no denying that a cleaning triathlon is a lot of work, but the results will be rewarding and assuredly worth the effort. If you can get the kids creatively involved you'll kill two birds with one stone. I actually found two dead birds in my hall closet last year. Granted, I've already trademarked the term, *The Spring Clean Triathlon*, but for a small fee I would be happy to send you a Spring Cleaning kit to get you started. We even have Spring Clean 2015 t-shirts in assorted colors and sizes. Think of the slogan possibilities, "Keep it Alive in 2-0-1-5, "Rad Dad and The #1 Clean Team" or more to the point, "Damn Right I'm Mean - Now Quit Whining and Clean." My mom would be so proud.

4 Spring has Sprung
The onset of Spring Fever

My family and I have recently been showing signs of an illness that is every bit as frightening as the Zika virus. Apparently, we're not the only family in the area afflicted with an atmospherically transmitted disease (ATD not to be confused with a STD), and it has the potential to turn into an outbreak that has The Center for Disease Control (CDC) on high alert. My exhaustive research (I made it up) indicates this current strain will probably last until school gets out for the summer in June. Symptoms include: lack of concentration, hyperactivity, sleep aversion, claustrophobia and the giggles. If you haven't guessed it already, the Copelands have been diagnosed with a severe case of Spring Fever. So far, the only known antidote is fresh air, loud music, a 7-Eleven Slurpee and fun.

After four drought-plagued years, we now have water in our reservoirs, snow pack in our mountains, and flowers in our gardens. I'm secure enough in my masculinity to admit that I like flowers. Tulips are my favorite if you must know. Anyone remotely familiar with Spring Fever knows that flowers often have a soothing/calming effect on the worst of cases. Exhaustive research (made it up again) has confirmed that flowers can subliminally increase many human's energy levels and supplement lacking pep and vigor. Apparently, exposure to annuals, perennials and blooming blossoms (not the Outback Steakhouse kind) can increase vitality, hope, optimism and a positive outlook, a provide a "spring in our step" if you will. That is unless of course you have allergies or hay fever, in which case you're a probably a flower hater. Don't be a hater!

In my professional opinion, flowers add vibrant color and a delightful visual contrast to our suburban landscape that last year consisted of dirt, dog poop, weeds and artificial lawn. Yes,

I have been known to exaggerate a bit, but without the recent abundance of precipitation, our I-680 corridor could've taken on the desolate cinematic look of the Academy-award winning *Mad Max Fury Road*.

Look around; thanks to the weather we've had this spring our hills and valleys are spectacular. Keeping with a movie theme, there are areas of the Tri-Valley that would be the perfect set location for a charming little romantic comedy entitled *Spring Fever* starring the devilishly handsome Ryan Reynolds and irresistible Julianne Hough. I envision them strolling along Prospect Avenue in downtown Danville, holding hands and window-shopping before lunching at Sideboard or reading a copy of *Alive* magazine over a latte at Pascal's. Note to self, begin drafting screen play. Soundtrack idea: The 1973 hit song by the Brady Bunch titled "It's a Sunshine Day." Anyone? Just me? Awkward.

More exhaustive research (again, made it up) says people between the ages of 3 and 74 years old prefer watching movies in 3D Technicolor on an IMAX screen as opposed to viewing an 8 mm black and white silent film in a closet. Pastel colored flower beds, emerald green hills, blooming white cherry blossoms, cresting blue lakes and a bright orange sun in the sky is what inspired Crayola to come up with all those crayon colors.

More exhaustive research (really, you have to ask?) has confirmed that one effective medicinal treatment for Spring Fever is apparently sports viewing. Fortunately for the afflicted, spring begins with the conclusion of March Madness, the NCAA basketball tournament. College B-ball transitions into the start of the major league baseball season. As MLB picks up momentum, we slide into the NBA and Hockey playoffs. Granted, professional basketball and hockey playoffs both seem to extend well into the summer months, but they can still provide medicinal benefits when the virus reaches a climax. Add a sprinkling of golf, tennis and soccer; it's all just a build up to my favorite spring sport medicine treatment, the NFL draft. The draft seems to bring my fever down better than two Advil and a picnic.

Spring has long been referred to as a prelude to summer, a summer tease. That's right, exhaustive research (of course I made it up) states that most people feel that the breezy cloud-filled days of April and May are preparing us for, or are a build up to, the warm days and star-filled nights of June, July and August. Flying kites, tending gardens and cleaning house are ideal ways to prep for family camp outs, company BBQs and neighborhood pool parties. Musically, spring is Kenny G and Christopher Cross where summer is more Def Leppard and Journey. Exhaustive research (I asked my daughters this time), says a more contemporary musical reference (something from the last decade) would be Taylor Swift, One Direction or Adele (Spring), and Fall Out Boy, Bruno Mars or Jason Aldean (Summer).

Spring Fever is rarely terminal, although it can certainly feel like you're dying a slow death if you're stuck in a classroom or office building on a beautiful sun-filled weekday afternoon. Adults are just as susceptible to the fever as kids. I've personally known at least two co-workers who have spent time in "treatment facilities" as the result of over-medicating the Spring Fever with margaritas and mojitos.

The secret to successfully dealing with the onset of the fever is to first recognize the fever's five "R" triggers: 1) Realize when you just can't stand to be indoors another second, 2) Respect the call of the outdoors, 3) Respond to the calling, 4) Reward yourself with an abundance of outdoor living, and 4) Rinse and wipe. Wipe? Sorry, wrong illness. 4) Repeat step 4 over and over again until exhausted. A little bit of spring fever can actually make your weekends so much more enjoyable and rewarding.

Spring Fever may not be curable, but it is treatable.

5 Beware of Hotel Hell
Poor accommodations can ruin a vacation

With the school year just about over, a lot of us are making summer vacation plans. Regardless if your travel plan is a visit with family and friends, or the itinerary includes an on-the-go sightseeing adventure or a relaxing destination vacation, you'll undoubtedly need overnight accommodations. It makes no difference if you travel by plane, train or automobile and end up at the beach, desert, big city or the mountains. Where you stay is almost as important as where you go.

I have had more than my share of bad hotel, motel, lodge, inn and resort experiences while traveling. I've stayed in places where serial killers wouldn't leave their victims. I've slept in rooms where CSI crime scene technicians refused to go. I've swum in a pool that was once a septic tank. I've eaten my free continental breakfast when the choices were broken waffle cones, decorated Easter eggs (in October) and expired powder milk. I've seen a maid using a leaf blower to clean a room, a desk clerk who was outfitted in a haz-mat suit and ironically, I once had a one-legged bellhop. I've seen banquet rooms hosting everything from a Scientology recruitment drive to a support group meeting for cross-dressing necrophilia hoarders. Finally, I've wondered if those were actually loose Raisinettes left on my pillow and bedspread by the "turn-down" service. Come to think of it, they were a little saltier than most Goober chocolates.

When I once worked for a company that was a little the cheap side, they insisted all of their sales reps stay at national discount motel chain. When I first arrived, the valet parking lot attendant moved my car off-site and rented it out by the hour. The hotel restaurant doubled as a soup kitchen and the bare-chested chef made the daily special in the Jacuzzi. The altar in the wedding chapel was equipped with a metal detector. Happy Hour in the hotel bar consisted of passing around a bottle of homemade bathtub wine wrapped in a brown paper bag. The workout room was fully equipped with a bent hula-hoop, chalk-drawn hopscotch court and a set of Buns of Steele VHS tapes. I did appreciate that I got a complimentary penicillin shot at every third stay, but I hated that check out was done at gunpoint. I heard that the Cave Dwellers Association ("CWA") rejected the hotel because the accommodations weren't up to CWA standards. The Chamber of Commerce proudly listed the venue as the only hazardous waste drop-off site in a 230-mile radius with overnight accommodations.

Once a year, my buddies and I do an annual boys road trip to enjoy a weekend of golf and "Hall Pass" merriment. Over the years, we've stayed in some pretty sketchy boardinghouses. It's a guy's getaway so we're not looking for a couples massages and sunset terraces, but I'm pretty a few of the places we've stayed were on the verge of being condemned. As we pulled into the parking lot last year, which resembled a bombed-out Syrian airport runway, the crime scene tape was still up blocking our way into the syringe littered lobby. We did appreciate that the concierge, who also handled room service, mani/pedi spa treatments and landscape maintenance, asked if we wanted to purchase a MMP card. The phone in our room had the Suicide Prevention Center on speed dial. The pool was a popular pet-washing destination until someone's lizard died from a bacterial infection. I understand that the check cashing bodega/adult bookstore/coin laundry down the street frequently complained that the motel guests brought down the image of the neighborhood and I'll admit many of the other patrons could easily have passed for squatters. At least they had Wi-Fi. The password was . . . "SaveMe."

The worst of my hotel stays may have been on my honeymoon. My worries began when I noticed that the sundry shop was stocked with bug bombs and rattraps. It wasn't so bad that our room had bunk beds, but we were disappointed that another couple had already claimed the bottom bed. Boy, were they noisy. We were hoping we might be upgraded to a room with carpeting or at the very least drapes, but no such luck. We found the gardener's severed finger in the ice machine, the vending machines sold ammunition and our wake-up call was the manager's wife leaning on her car horn. It resembled a youth hostel without all the warmth and amenities. The blacklight app on my phone made it abundantly clear that the room had at one time been used as a porn set. Our first clue should have been the brochure that suggested visitors bring their own soap, shampoo and fly swatter.

Often, bed & breakfast establishments aren't any better. For our anniversary, we stayed at a B&B near the delta and the sign at the entrance proudly stated, *#1 Destination for Conjugal Visits.* The maid was attempting to change the sheets in our room when we arrived, but she had trouble prying them apart. The mini-bar consisted of a glass of tap water and a few opened bags of airline peanuts. The complimentary happy hour offered a choice of either hillbilly moonshine or a nice Bartles & James wine cooler flight from 1982-84, however the plastic glasses all had lipstick stains. The adult movie selection turned out to be hidden cameras set up in the adjoining rooms. While it was pet friendly, most of the dogs chose to sleep in the car after seeing the raccoon gang hanging out next to the kitchen dumpsters. The good news was there were plenty of those salty Raisinettes virtually everywhere.

I'm quite certain there are those of you reading this article who are non-believers. Those who think I'm making this all up for the sake of another hilariously funny, laugh out loud/can't put down humor lifestyle magazine article. To that I say, "What?" Much like the Extended Limited Express security guard said, aka homeless guy who offered to watch our shi . . . stuff while we waited for our handi-capable van ride back to the airport, "I may not have much, but I have my integrity (and a 24-oz. can of Schlitz Malt Liquor)." If you can't afford to stay at the Ritz Carlton, Four Seasons or Fairmont, a word to the wise: do your due diligence when it comes to where you'll be staying. Otherwise, you might just be setting your self up for a visit to Hotel Hell.

Comedy is Serious Business
My 5 Minutes of Stand-Up

Last night, Wednesday night, July 8th, I performed a five-minute set of stand-up comedy at Tommy T's Comedy Club in Pleasanton. My good friend and comedy mentor, David VanAvermaete, talked me into "The Stand-Up Experience" as the premise for this very article. As invigorating as it was last night, I still feel like I might throw up.

"Teaching Mike stand-up comedy is somewhat like teaching a bird to fly. Assuming the bird is a penguin." —DVA

When David initially told me he would be producing a show and brought up the idea, my immediate response was, "Let me think about it . . . No!" Doing a live stand-up comedy routine on stage was never on my bucket list. I'll admit that I like attention and the spotlight as much as the next guy (OK, more than the next guy), but utter humiliation is not how I envision getting it. David assured me that under his tutelage, I would craft a set worthy of applause and laughter. Hence began my crash course in Stand-Up 101.

"This could be a springboard for Mike to explore other forms of comedy. Mime comes to mind." —DVA

Prior to our first meeting, David had me write out a word-for-word set. I then performed it for him at his home in San Ramon one sunny day in June. He provided me with techniques on structure, conceptual formula (keep the jokes about myself and my life), word placement and pacing. We met once a week for three weeks as I tightened the content, flow and timing of my set. I was still tweaking my material right up until show time, which probably hurt me because I forgot a few key jokes once up on stage.

"Mike's set started off slow and then tapered off." —DVA

The lineup for last night's show featured emcee Ben Feldman, who opened and performed for 15 minutes. That was followed by my short set of five minutes. After me, Michael Slack did 15 minutes, followed by featured act Anthony Hill who did twenty minutes. Headliner David VanAvermaete performed a modified version of his full set (thirty minutes). The other comedians, now that I can technically call myself a comedian, were incredibly welcoming and supportive. I had met Anthony Hill previously and his encouragement was very heartfelt. I am a big fan of Anthony and last night he was trying out quite a bit of new material, not all of which drew big laughs. Anthony's ability to roll with the crowd's tepid response and "transition" was inspiring.

"When Mike went up on the stage an anticipatory hush came over the crowd. Unfortunately, the hush persisted well into his set." —DV

"Fortunately, several audience members accidentally laughed . . . when they got their bill." —DVA

There were approximately eighty people in the crowd at Tommy T's for the show and a few were close friends and family of mine. Their support (and forced laughter) was very much appreciated. I really wasn't as nervous as one might expect, probably because I was focused on not forgetting my lines. Below is an excerpt from my set.

As you heard, this is my first time onstage and I'll admit to being nervous. Hopefully my first joke won't involve me crapping my pants, although that would be funny....to you.

I'm so green I didn't even know what to wear tonight. Someone suggested something to make me look younger and thinner so I went over to Macys at the mall and asked them to direct me to their catfish and pedophile department.

Much to my surprise, they had one.

This is my joke set list, which I'm going to place on this stool. It's there to help me find my place just in case I get lost or have a panic attack.

Or pass out from Vertigo.

This stage is a lot higher than the last stage I appeared on, that being the coffee table in our family room. I sure miss my lucky American Girl Doll mic right about now.

For those you who don't know me, my name is Mike Copeland. I am 52 years old, but I've been told by a lot of people that I don't look a day over 60.

They never tell you as a kid that the first two things to go on an aging white male are hair and butt and I don't know which one is receding faster?

My hair started too recede when I was about thirty one or thirty two...months old.

"Receding' is probably an understatement. The definition of recede is to retreat, well my hair line has retreated all the way down to my shoulders. I think we can all agree that my hairline has finally surrendered.

The good news is a local plastic surgeon has asked me to be their "after" photo for their new butt reduction procedure.

I guess it could be worse. Loose fitting jeans and the lack of a pocket comb are better than the alternative, that being the 3 "I" words; incompetence, incontinence and impotence.

I am married, sorry ladies. Just like the steak here at Tommy T's, this boner in Rib Eye is off the menu.

21 years ago I was sentenced to life and ever since, I've been

doing time at the suburban slow death penitentiary.

I kid. My wife is here tonight and she has a great sense of humor, however if I read her body language correctly there goes any hope for a "conjugal visit".

I bet tonight as we get ready for be there may be a role reversal to our little game. I'll probably end up being the guard and she'll be the prisoner who's just been executed by lethal injection.

I have two beautiful teenage daughters, thank you again for that sympathetic round of applause.

I'm kind of proud to say that within their peer group, I'm the cool dad.

Probably because I buy them and their friends pot, beer and cigarettes.

I'm only kidding, I don't buy them cigarettes.

I love my daughters and they love their.... cell phones, debit cards and anything WiFi.

As you heard during my intro, I am writer. Most of the magazines I write for don't offer home delivery, but you can these periodicals in local bookstores in section entitled, "FREE, Take One."

Currently, I'm with ALIVE magazine. It's a lot like *Vanity Fair* or *The New Yorker* in that it's got a front cover, back cover and pages with words and pictures.

I write a humor lifestyle column, and I'm pretty sure I know what a lot of you are thinking right now......When did Tommy's have steak on the menu?

The rest of you are probably thinking, "He writes humor? Why not write about what you know more about, like humiliation?"

I'm not certain that my writing will translate from the page to the stage, as I find that I'm at my most hilarious when I'm sitting alone in my home office late at night, pant less.

I find that by not wearing pants, I'm less inhibited, more

relaxed and the creative juices are free flowing.

Unfortunately, Tommy has a "Must Wear Pants on Stage" policy.

I suppose if I was Jerry Seinfeld he might waive that policy. *Seinfeld impression*: What's the deal with pants? I'm not wearing them!?

When it comes to impressions, I've been told my Jerry Seinfeld sounds a lot like Jerry Seinfeld imitating Don Knotts during a prostate exam.

In addition to my magazine writing, I have two books in publication. I'm proud to tell you that they are currently on the bestseller list ...at the *Trunk of My Car Bookstore*.

We have one convenient location . . . wherever I am.

I had a bit about a recent traffic incident being the result of "Roid Rage"—hemorrhoids, not steroids. I surmised that anal fissures were the cause of Dr. David Banner's metamorphoses into the Hulk, but it wasn't really coming together and caused my set to run long. There was also a joke about getting advice from the employees at Tommy T's immediately following their employee comedy competition, Last Busboy Standing. This bit lacked punchlines. My big ending was a joke about my dogs and some of their inappropriate behavior, but it's not really suitable for a family magazine and I forgot half of it when I was up on stage.

"Just when you thought it couldn't get any less funny, Mike launched into some impersonations." —DVA

"For a first timer, Mike had great poise and pretty good timing. He gave the impression he had done this at least once before." —Scot Wilson

"I've seen worse comics who performed for longer. Mike got some respectable laughs." —Derek Sousa

I liken the whole stand-up experience to skydiving. The first time I tandem jumped, the adrenaline was pumping and it was exhilarating, but it was somewhat of a surreal blur. The second time I jumped, I was completely in the moment and it was so much more rewarding. Performing stand-up comedy takes a lot more courage than skydiving, but I would consider doing another five-to-seven minute set in the future hoping to absorb it all slightly better. 1 guess I could always turn my house into a comedy club (Mikey C's) for a night and do my routine from our family room coffee table with my lucky American Girl Doll karaoke mic. Thank you, I'll be here all week. Two shows; nine and eleven, don't forget to tip your waitresses.

"Watching Mike do comedy is like finding a condom in your teenage son's wallet – awkward and embarrassing, mixed with a little pride." —DVA

"My best advice to Mike is to taper off his performance schedule over the next 4 weeks and then quit altogether." —DVA

Summer Writer's Block Party – Vol. 1

I'm blocked! Creatively, not digestively. Although come to think of it, I haven't been very regular for the past few weeks. I suppose one thing could have something to do with the other, but I digress. I always seem to have trouble coming up with something new to write about for our summer issues. Knowing that my deadlines are roughly four to six weeks before publication, it makes sense that given the time of year I'm undoubtedly feeling the effects of "spring fever." Just like our kids start tweaking for summer vacation once the days get longer and the temperature warms up, I must be experiencing something similar. Maybe it's something we never outgrow, even though I'm lucky if I get one week off from work in mid-July unlike the ten-week respite from school my so-called children enjoy.

In years past, my summer articles have ranged from summer relevant topics such as the end of school ("School's Out," "June Swoon," "Sizzling Summers"), to summer vacations ("My Summer Vacations," "Our Trip to the Moon," "We're going to Euroland"). Local day trips ("The Last Daze of Summer"), to swim team ("The Obsession with Swim Team") and back-to-school ("The Back to School Experience" and "Sentenced to Another Year"). Then, when I'm struggling for material, the subject matter has wandered into our community ("Suburban Superhero"), my run-ins with famous people ("I've Met Famous People"), self-indulgence ("My Interview with Me") and my envy of all things canine ("I Wish I was a Dog"). Admittedly, I tend to reach when I can't come up with anything topical or tropical. For some reason, my creative brilliance is overflowing when the weather turns chilly and it gets dark around 4:50 pm., but the minute I put on my True Religion cut-off jeans, One Direction tank-top and Tory Burch sandals, my brain turns to mush.

Typically, when I run into a bout of writer's block, I play a word association game to help stimulate ideas. If I throw out enough word keys one of them is bound to unlock the door to my right brain.

"I am the Right Brain. I am creativity. A free spirit. I am passion. Yearning. Sensuality. I am the sound of roaring laughter. I am taste. The feeling of sand beneath bare feet and rain upon my head. I am movement and dance. Vivid colors. I am the urge to paint on an empty canvas. I am boundless imagination. I am art and poetry. I sense, I feel, I explore."

Sadly, I stole that description of the right brain from somewhere, but it helps paint the picture. I like to start with the term, "writer's block" and free associate from there. OK, writer's block. Go!

Writer's words... yeah, I got nothing. Writers writing.... again nothing. Writer's right brain, it's already been done (see above). Maybe I should get away from the word <u>writer</u> and focus on <u>block</u> – Block head ... Charlie Brown ©, block of cheese ... I like cheese, blocks are for babies ... babies can't write, block party ... neighbors, chillaxing, food, music, talking, drinking, etc. I think I can work with this. Something's coming to me. The creative juices are flowing. My right brain is churning. Here comes the purge, baby.

Summer block parties can be a great time spent with neighbors and friends. A time to come out of our houses and bond together as the micro community after too many months sequestered inside. In reality, it's not unusual to literally go months at a time without seeing many of our neighbors during the long and harsh California winters. I'm pretty sure it rained at least twelve days between November and April. Ok, maybe it's not the weather that keeps us from interacting, but the truth is with fewer daylight hours, a lot of us are on the road before the sun comes up and don't get home until way past sunset. That and I'm also pretty sure one of my neighbors (who shall remain nameless, Ed Leonard) hibernates all winter. There's no hard proof that he sleeps from Thanksgiving until roughly Easter, but that gut and beard aren't helping his "I've been traveling a lot for work" argument. If done right, a block party can bring out the apparent agoraphobics (Lofbaum family), can help those that have trouble engaging in neighborly conversation (Dr. Leon Roth) and even mend fences due to some small riff (Guy Nadivi suspected Jerry Wiener of stealing his *Maxim* magazines). At worst, it's a chance to enjoy a libation or twelve (Debbie Malin) with friends. Once the tables are set up and the grilling begins, good times are usually had by all. The cool thing about a pot luck block party is that everyone contributes to the communal table; chips and dip, fruit bowls and veggie platters, jello shots, hot dogs and hamburgers, desserts, beer/wine and margaritas. It's just like in the book *Rock Pasta*, or was it a movie?"

"Stone Soup is an old folk story in which hungry strangers persuade local people of a town to give them food. It is usually told as a lesson in cooperation, especially amid scarcity. In varying traditions, the stone has been replaced with other common inedible objects, and therefore the fable is also known as button soup, wood soup, nail soup, and axe soup. It is an Aarne Thompson tale circa 1548. Thanks Mr. Wikipedia.

At our recent block party, I noticed that a few of my neighbors looked like they haven't seen the sun in a while. Either that or they're vampires. This is Danville, California, not Forks, Washington. A block party can often time lead to a pool party. Now that's what I'm talking about! Here's a chance to lather up with a sunscreen (given the fact that I'm follicle challenged, SPF 6000 is my brand) and chill in my water wings by the old cement pond. We had a pool our house until the dog bit a hole in it.

Getting back to the block party, so much of the fun is catching up with the people that share our little slice of suburbia. We may each have individual homes, but we do essentially live together. In the prehistoric days, clusters of families were known as a clan and the clan usually lived in blocks of cave neighborhoods (much like the Flintstones and Rubbles). Everyone had a role within the clan that was integral of the group's basic survival needs of food, shelter and clothing. Back then, no one cared if the Zimmet's lawn wasn't mowed as long as the Mrs. Zimmet could skin a bison. Of course, that was during *Clan of the Cave Bear* times. Today HOAs have rules. Do you hear me Zimmet? How about pulling the Toro out of the garage this weekend and mowing down those corn stalks in your front yard?

The Clan of the Cave Bear is a historical novel by Jean M. Auel about prehistoric times. It examines clan culture and speculates on the possibilities of interactions between Neanderthal and modern Cro-Magnon humans. A great summer time read.

The young and virile men on our block party would have hunted wholly mammoth together, while the women folk cared for the children and tended the garden. The older and wiser neighbors might have built tools, painted hieroglyphics on the cave walls and taken on roles such as medicine man/woman. I'm pretty sure several neighbors have their medical marijuana cards. I just can't determine who amongst us is smart enough to discover fire or the wheel, but it's probably not me (or Rick Simmons). My jobs would probably entail communicating with other clans and determining where to dig the poop hole?

When you think about it, prehistoric neighborhood clans had a block party virtually every day of the year since they shared most meals together, prayed together, entertained together and bathed together. This is likely the origination of today's version of a block party, minus the bathing part. Unless you live in the Shadow Creek development, I've heard their after-hours block spa parties can get pretty darn crazy.

Look at that, 1,363 words about writer's block and a neighborhood block party. Damn, I'm good.

8 Summer Writer's Block – Vol. 2

It's here again. I find myself afflicted with that dreaded summer writer's block and the first symptom is constipation of my creative orifice. In layman's terms, for you non-professional writers in the magazine audience, I just can't think of a doggone thing to write about for September's end of summer/beginning of fall issue. As most of you know, I suffered from this same ailment last year and out of absolutely nowhere I came up with an incredibly entertaining article on our neighborhood block parties entitled "Summer Writer's Block Party." I'm so darn talented I impress myself sometimes.

But, alas that was last year. This year . . . I got nothing. The past few weeks I've been asking everyone (wife, kids, co-workers, mailman—he sure seems to be around a lot, and the milkman. I didn't even know there was such a thing as a milkman anymore and he sure resembles the mailman), but no one came up with any suggestions, ideas, interesting stories or even a colorful haiku? I love a good haiku.

Perhaps the way to go about this is to simply compile a sampling of ramblings. I see it in the newspaper all the time. When a writer doesn't have enough material for an entire article, he/she assembles a collection of short blurbs, dare I say vignettes, on a variety of topics to make his/her deadline with the required word count. I could do that. Here goes nothing.

Dreaming: I've been dreaming a lot lately. Get your mind out of the gutter. These are harmless PG-13 dreams. Maybe my nocturnal dreamscape is due to the warm summer nights or the Peyote toothpaste I've been using? Either way, I often wake up drenched in a cold sweat having just dreamt that I was running from someone trying to kill me. Coincidently, it's usually our handsome mail/milkman. My kids tell me they've also been dreaming a lot more than usual, probably about how they're going to adjust to a new dad who has two labor- intensive delivery jobs. Even our dogs seem to be dreaming, however their dreams are likely connected to five-pound steak bones, peeing in every yard in Danville or hopefully biting the mail/milkman.

There are all kinds of websites to help us interpret our dreams. Check out www.dreammoods.com, www.dreamforth.com, www.dream-dictionary.org or www.dreams.com. I'm a little reluctant to have my dreams interpreted for fear of what it could tell me, starting with my insecurity about delivery men.

Kickin' it: Growing up, kickball was one of my favorite summertime games. For those of you unfamiliar with this totally awesome competitive sport, it's a unique blend of softball, soccer, dodge ball and Hunger Games. On any given summer day, the kids in our neighborhood would assemble and teams would be drafted. If I happened to be selected a captain it would go something a little like this; "I'll take Terry Ivie, Laura Faravelli, Victor Martina and the Mocking Jay - Katniss Everdeen." To start to play, the pitcher would roll a hard rubber ball to the batter and that person would kick the ball. If someone caught it in the air the batter was out. If the ball bounced along the ground the fielders had to pick it up and throw it at a runner. If they hit the runner before that person reached a base they were out. If the runner eluded the thrown ball they were awarded the base. The offense scored runs the traditional way, every time a runner crossed home plate. However, in our neighborhood, the defense could score points by throwing the ball so hard a runner was knocked down, or if the runner cried, or in the event of a decapitation. I've convinced our old neighborhood has such a disproportionately high level of adult homelessness and unemployment due to the long term effects of kickball-related concussion syndrome.

Alive and Kickin' it: I've only sold approximately 17.5 copies of my latest book, *Alive and Chillin'* My first book, *Alive and Kickin'*, sold well into the twenties. Granted, Kickin' is probably more appealing than Chillin', but now I'm a little depressed? A good game of kickball would probably get me out of my funk, but now that all my buddies are in their early 50's someone would undoubtedly break a hip. I was truly hoping my book would be released last December so I could capitalize on the holiday gift buying season. Unfortunately, we had to push out the release date due to complicated publishing issues. I couldn't find anyone to like my book and give a positive testimonial. I've seen people post photos of their feet and get fifty "Likes" on Facebook. Hoping to take advantage of the Valentine gift buying season, we tried to drop the book in February, but sadly that didn't happen either. The book finally came out in May, but the Memorial Day gift buying season did not generate the sales we anticipated. I'm hoping for a back-to-school gift buying push or I'll be handing out signed copies to trick-or-treaters on Halloween.

Fear of Flying: I've done a fair amount of air travel these last few months, for business and pleasure, but I'm not what you would consider a frequent flyer. First Class and Business are too pricy for me so I typically travel in the coach section. Lately, due to all the mergers and acquisitions in the airline industry, I've had occasion to travel in "Going out of Business" class. You don't get all the perks and benefits of actual Business Class, but you can really negotiate a great deal on the faire. The seats are about as roomy as a high school math desk and to be honest, I get a little tired of the Kirkland brand drinks and snacks, but at least the seat-back televisions in GOOB Class offer a reasonably good selection of '80s Beta and VHS tapes. *Meatballs, Strips, St. Elmo's Fire* and (Who ya gonna call?) *Ghostbusters*!

Higher Education: I recently decided to further my education by getting a degree online. I liked the idea of working toward my advanced studies at my own pace in the comfort of my own home. However, things started going wrong right away. First I didn't get into the online dorms. I got my housing application in late and now I have to look for off campus cloud housing. Next, I got cyber bullied when I rushed a virtual fraternity. Those guys from Apple Dell Toshiba (ADT) are real jerks. Finally, my twenty-two-year-old test proctor put me on academic probation when I had an unexplained absence during my final exam. Unexplained? I had to give the kids their lunch money and sign for a Fed Ex delivery. Now I have to do 150 hours of web based community service before I can get my e-diploma. I'm considering dropping out of school.

I've got more material on everything from recycled water fill-up stations to Donald Trump and the pre-election election, but frankly I'm exhausted and want to take a nap. All in all, I'd say this article is better than nothing unless of course there's a general consensus that nothing might have been better? I promise to come back with something stronger in the next issue. Something that's seasonal, topical or spiritually uplifting. Anybody have any ideas?

Summer Writer's Block – Vol. 3

It's not a big surprise that my annual summer writer's block is back. I've come to expect it. When summer rolls around, every orifice in my body tightens up when it's time to extract something creative for this fine magazine. I've found it tough coming up with magic when I'm wearing flip-flops and board shorts while sucking on a cold Corona. Truthfully, after 9+ years of at least one article a month, the well might finally be dry. Brilliance is fleeting. Truthfully, I may have peaked in the spring of 2011. As NBA announcer and former Golden State Warriors Head Coach Mark Jackson once said (when the team got bounced from the playoffs too early), "There's no shame in my game." Well, there's no game in my shame either or something like that. I came, I wrote and now I'm tired. I don't want to talk retirement just yet, but similar to last summer, the best that I can do right now is come up with a few random thoughts on a variety of unrelated topics.

College Bound
My oldest daughter, Hannah, is leaving for college in a couple of weeks and I'm sad. I'm happy for her, but sad for me. Me, I'm probably going to cry. I'm very close with my girls and not having the oldest one around will take some getting used to, and I'm not sure I'm ready. Granted, every baby bird leaves the nest eventually, but my guess is it's easier for the mommy bird to adjust than the daddy bird. Mommy birds are tougher and they had to sit on those damn eggs forever. Not to mention regurgitating three meals a day for months. Now I'll have to focus 100% of my attention on her younger sister, Claire. How was school today? What did you do at school? Do you like your teachers? Who did you hang with/talk to/text? Do you have a lot of home-

work? What are your plans for the weekend? Do you want to walk the dog with me? Watch TV with me? Go to the gym with me? Let's bake cookies. Hopefully I'll be able to hang on until Parents' Weekend at the University of Colorado (Sept. 30th - Oct. 2nd) without first having a major breakdown. Whatever you do, don't even remind me that both my girls will be going away this time next year because I don't think my heart can take it. I'm thinking of starting The Danville Lonely Dad's Club. Applications are available online at www.lonelydads.com.

Olympic Blues

I love the Olympics. There are over 10,000 athletes representing 205 countries (minus a few who have been banned for PED doping). It's the thrill of international competition, the amazing athletic accomplishments and the immense pride of country that inspires me every four years. It inspires me to go into rehab after watching approximately 280 hours of television over a two-week period. I just can't seem to get enough swimming and diving, track & field, gymnastics, rowing and fencing. What am I going to do with all my spare time once the Olympic committee wraps up the closing ceremonies? I guess I could pick up a hobby like ballroom dancing, magic or binge watch *Game of Thrones*. I've heard *Game of Thrones* is a little Olympic-like, if Olympic events included slayings, incest and dragon defecation.

Happy Viewing

If *Game of Thrones* is too big a commitment, *Silicon Valley* and *Veep* might be the right call. These two HBO sitcoms are quite possibly the funniest two shows on television. That is, if you don't mind an occasional F-bomb in the dialogue. By occasional, I mean virtually every other word. Regardless, both of these shows are uniquely crafted, wonderfully acted and perfectly paced if you like that sort of thing. *Silicon Valley* follows the rise, fall and VC flogging of a data compression start-up located in Sun River, Oregon. Just kidding, the company, Pied Piper, is located in Silicon Valley…pay attention! *Veep*, on the other hand, is about a female Vice President and her staff of politically gifted, but morally challenged, gutter-mouthed nitwits. Serena Meyer maneuvers Capitol Hill as the Assistant President (VEEP) for three seasons before ascending to the position of POTUS, President of the United States in Season Four. The brilliance of both shows is in the writing. Something I can relate to, obviously. The rapid-fire in both *Silicon Valley* and *Veep* sparkles with topical references, industry accuracy and jaw-dropping insults, putdowns and trash-talking. If only I could employ that type of banter in my work place. I hope the writers of these two shows can keep it up because, take it from someone who knows, it's difficult to be brilliant for an extended period of time.

Book Club

I don't belong to a book club, but I'm open to an invitation. If I did belong to one, my first recommendation would be *The Magic Strings of Frankie Presto* by Mitch Albom. You might recognize the author's name from his previous works, which include *Tuesdays with Morrie, The Five People You Meet in Heaven* and *For One More Day*. While technically I can label myself a writer, I'm not a Mitch Albom type of writer. He's in a completely different league than yours truly. Using baseball vernacular, Mitch is first ballot Hall of Famer, 300-game winner and I'm a single-A utility infielder that makes a lot of errors. The above-referenced book chronicles the life of a guitar virtuoso from birth to death with Forrest Gump type run-ins with actual musicians such as Duke Ellington, Elvis, Hank Williams, Burt Bacharach, Lyle Lovett and Paul Stanley of Kiss. It includes a love story, a reunited family story and a music history story. From cover to cover, it's a wonderful compelling read. The type of writing a hack magazine scribe can only dream about penning. One day.

Dub Nation

I've been a Golden State Warriors fan since the early '70s and the addition of Kevin Durant to an already great team, still hasn't sunk in. I saw my first game in 1975, the fall after they won their first NBA Championship and to be honest, I truly never thought I would see the team win another one. The 2014-15 season was a dream come true and the conclusion of the 2015-16 season was a nightmare. Now, with Durant, they might not lose a game next season. If you thought 73 wins was impressive just wait until they rip off 16 straight playoff wins in a row. Just kidding, the Dub's might lose one game, if they rest the starters. However, they might also run off five or six titles in a row. Wouldn't that be awesome? Rub-a- Dub-Dub, four All-Stars in a tub.

Military Man

Best wishes go out to my wife's cousin, Robert Scharff, who is serving our country in the army. He is stationed somewhere overseas and in all likelihood in harm's way. Don't forget our loyal service men and women who keep our country safe and secure. It's the home of the free because of the brave. Stay safe Robbie, our hearts and prayers are with you.

I do like these compilation pieces, although a few of the haters might see them as pieces of dog excrement. I like dogs so I can give anything a positive spin. Hopefully next month, I'll regain my mojo and come up with an entire article on just one topic. Either that or I'll formally retire from my ten-hour-a-month volunteer writing job and travel the world. Just kidding, I can't afford to travel the world. Who do I look like, Mark

Zuckerberg? If you did like this article, please like it on my Facebook page and maybe MZ will hire me to be Vice President of Humor Lifestyle at FB or the official FB Humor Lifestyle blogger. The stock options alone would cure my writer's block.

10 Summer Writer's Block – Vol. 4

Yes, if you're keeping score at home, this is my 4th summer of writer's constipation. As both of my loyal readers know, I struggle each year with something to write about at the conclusion of my summer vacation season. Sadly, "vacation" this year ultimately means moving my daughters to their respective colleges, (pause for a heavy sigh), and not tanning in my sexy Speedo swimsuit at some far away, yet affordable, sun soaked destination spot like Lodi or Copperopolis.

At the beginning of the summer, I set three goals for myself; #1, Spend quality time with my daughters (without driving them crazy), #2, Eradicate (painfully) the gopher gang wreaking havoc on my backyard landscape and #3, Try to somehow strike a stronger resemblance to my younger, thinner and more handsome Bitmoji. I had also hoped to craft a Summer Writer's Block piece that informed and entertained the ALIVE audience with a splattering of offerings related to my current surroundings. This is more a mission statement than a goal.

Prognostication - If anyone out there in readerville remembers my 2016 Summer Writer's Block Vol. 3 piece, I predicted the Warriors would go 81-1 in the regular season and 16-0 in the playoffs. It would appear that I wasn't too far off. My bookie thought I was nuts, but happily took my money, when I laid down that bet in late September 2016. Granted, I was a little nervous when the Dub's lost that first game of the season against the Spurs, which then required them to go 81-0 the balance of the season for me to collect, but I didn't feel it was impossible. Alas, I'm just happy Steph, Clay, Dray and KD brought the NBA championship back to the Bay Area even if I didn't win any money. Next year, I might wager on 200 points in a game (every game). Unfortunately, my Giants vs. A's World Series bet isn't looking overly strong right now, but there's still time and anything can happen.

Speaking of sports...
A Switch - This month, I'll be trading in two teenage girls for 40 tween-age boys. Beginning August 1st, I'll be once again coaching the junior midget (11-13 years old/90 - 150 lbs.) Division of San Ramon Valley Thunderbird football. Along with Head Coach Sean Gann, OC - Scott Harper, DC - Eric Nystrom and position coaches Rob Rutchena, George Schramm and Dave Stallard, (and numerous other coaches at the five separate divisions) we're out to turn boys into men...or at least into big boys. Full-pad tackle football is a huge time commitment consisting of conditioning, contact drills and playbook comprehension. The players have some work to do too. I can't give these young men enough credit because when a majority of their peers are glued to a video screen during the last few weeks of summer vacation, T-Bird players are working hard (physically and mentally) in ninety plus degree heat to compete at the ultimate team sport. I am undoubtedly biased, but it's hard to dispute that football builds character, integrity and camaraderie with your teammates that is hard to match playing Mind Craft or watching TV.

Speaking of watching TV...
Binge and Purge Watching - I just wrapped up binge watching House of Cards, Bloodline and Orange is the New Black. That was preceded by 13 Reasons Why, Stranger Things and old episodes of The West Wing. Now that *I've* digested all of those TV calories, I need to purge something. Perhaps, there's a television laxative I could take to clean out the viewing bowels. I can't wait to hurl out Chicago Fire, Chicago PD and Chicago Med. I would *have* completely blown out Chicago Justice, but luckily it only lasted one season. Fortunately, thanks to counseling, I'm

currently digesting a more reasonable serving of Veep, Silicon Valley and reruns of Modern Family. Maybe I should think about reading a book.

Speaking of books...

The Trilogy - People in the street are constantly approaching me, asking when I'll be coming out with my third book. First, they ask me for spare change or if I want to buy some weed, but then they ask about the book. SPOILER ALERT: The third leg of my trilogy is in the works, but I need another year's worth of material before I can reach the required 300-pages of dribble/er, content. I always knew my book series wouldn't be complete until the third installment came out. Much like Hunger Games, Divergent, Girl with the Dragon Tattoo and the 50 Shades of Gray series, it takes three books to tell the entire story of Mike Copeland. That and I am a sucker for the concept of self-publishing, self-promoting and maintaining my high self-esteem. Now if I could just get my former school library's to carry my books.

Speaking of school...

Grad Party Burnout. My wife and I attended our share of high school, college and 8th Grade graduation celebrations this summer not to mention going to a few away/farewell parties. One might say I *have* a grad party hangover or perhaps a hangover from being over served at every grad party we attended. Now that we are two-time veterans of the grad party wars, I feel the need to share a few valuable grad party tips or grad party Do's and Don'ts, if you will. **Do** hire a mobile caterer to handle the food - my recommendation is El Paisa Taco Truck from Oakland. The food is out of this world. **Don't** feel the need to throw back a shot of tequila with every guest that walks through the door. Bad choice. **Do** start making your plans ahead of time and not the night before. Been there/done that = gradtastrophy. I'm trying to talk my wife into hiring herself out as a Grad Party Consultant next year. If you're looking to outsource the stress of organizing a raging grad party, she would coordinate the food, booze, music, games, decorations and favors for you. She has experience and references (me). Book now for the 2018 graduation season, or Dec. of 2017 if your child happens to be graduating from trade school, cosmetology school or the exotic dancer academy. You can pay her in taco truck bucks. I *love* that gosh-darn food.

Speaking of high school...

Heart Felt Home Town Recognition. Sadly, I recently attended a funeral for perhaps the greatest athlete my high school (the original Mountain View High School on Castro Street in Mountain View, CA) ever produced. Denny Mateo was not only an incredible three-sport athlete, he was also an exemplary husband, father, brother, son, teammate and friend. Denny was a larger-than-life quarterback who had just led our small, military-base fed, ethnically-diverse high school to a Central Coast Section (CCS) Football Championship his sophomore year. Denny's hard working, humble, non-assuming demeanor was something everyone at our high school respected, and it proved to be a leadership lesson for players to come. He truly cared about people and his compassion inspired people. Denny was also the older brother of two of my close high school friends, Chris and Tim, and the son of my former coach (Mr. Dennis Mateo). Denny was someone special and my heart goes out to the entire family for their loss.

It seems I've lost too many friends my age the past few years. Joe Baker, Sean Cooley, Mark Fox, Ted Helgans and Pat McCarthy are all missed. It goes without saying that we all need to appreciate the time we have with the ones we love. In the immortal words of Rod Stewart, *Life is so brief and time is a thief... and like a fistful of sand it can slip right through your hands.* Live, Love, Laugh are good words to live by, especially if you're struggling with an imaginary case of summer writer's block.

11 Summer Writer's Block – Vol. 5

I've got a splitting headache from banging my head against my computer screen trying to think of something to write for the August issue of *ALIVE*. Sadly, I had hoped the blunt force trauma would spurn some new ideas, but alas, it's only triggered more concussion-like symptoms. What was I saying? This writer's block thing seems to happen every year around this time. After a couple family vacations, some crazy 4th of July shenanigans and a block party or two (#culetdrive), my creative tank has run out of gas. Plus, once you're over 50, most men struggle with memory issues. To be completely honest, I can't remember what I had for breakfast let alone what I've written about over the last ten years, unless I access my massive article scrapbook. Yes, I scrapbook. Don't judge me.

As many of you know, if I'm away on assignment, the Chief (aka Eric Johnson) has at times rerun a former article because there's not a real high likelihood a lot of current *ALIVE* readers actually saw or read the article when it originally came out. I'm only guessing since I never get any reader feedback. While I'm on that topic, my ALIVE email address must be printed incorrectly as it's been approximately twenty-seven months since I received any fan mail. Suffice it to say, and I do love saying "suffice it," I could probably rerun Summer's Writer's Block Volumes 1-4 and be relatively safe no one has read them; however, I have way too much integrity for those type of shenanigans. ("Shenanigans" is my new favorite word.) So, without further ado, the following is my annual collection of random summer thoughts instead of a long rambling piece on one specific subject or topic. Buckle up, it's going to be a bumpy ride.

Age Appropriate Attire: If you're a man over fifty, you really shouldn't be wearing a tank top/muscle T, ripped jeans, a team jersey with another man's name on it or your ball cap turned backwards. You look ridiculous. There, I said it. "Sun's out/guns out" is a fashion statement that should only be used by younger men like Zac Efron (28), Jimmy Garoppolo (26), Michael B. Jordan (29), or Jake (13), the kid who mows our lawn. As a sophisticated gentleman in my mid-50s, much like George Clooney pre-scooter accident, my wardrobe compliments my rocking Dad-bod. My lounge-wear is a little more stylish and laid back than my work attire, but I don't try to front like some British fancy man in his 30's. *The Idle Man* publication says men over 50 should focus on fit and colors, with a splash of accessories, rather than trends. Sage advice, which is why I shop at Forever 51 and buy sensible shoes at Nordstrom (for their generous return policy). Ultimately, my strategy is to dress my age and have my colors done.

Social Media Awareness – If you're a man over fifty, you really shouldn't be on Snapchat, Instagram or even Twitter. You look ridiculous. There, I said it. Stick with Facebook, LinkedIn, Pinterest and Foursquare like the rest of us dinosaurs. Leave the other sites to the millennial generation. "Snap me" is a term that should only be used by Justin Bieber (24), Draymond Green (28) or Palmer Luckey (23)—Google him. As a tech-challenged suburban gentleman, I stick to what I know and what I know is Open Table, Words with Friends, and on occasion, Fandango. They may not be social media sites, but they allow me to be social with my friends, family and co-workers. You won't find me on Tinder, but please don't hesitate to "Friend Me" and like my crazy kitten posts on Facebook.

Giving is Living: If you're a man over fifty, you really should spend some time volunteering. The second half of life should include giving back to your community. Sharing is caring. There, I said it. Once your kids are at an age where they don't need/want you around like they did when they were younger, there is a tendency to get sad, lonely and bored. All are terms that I relate to as an empty nest dad myself. One surefire way to overcome these understandably normal emotions is to volunteer and there are countless volunteer opportunities all around us. As a way to fill my empty hours, I've done everything from a single shift at the Alameda County Food Bank to coaching several seasons with the San Ramon Valley T-Birds. Volunteering is an easy and fulfilling way to spend time with incredible people doing something worthwhile. The SPCA is always looking for pet friends, East Bay Regional Park District has monthly trail rejuvenation projects and the annual Run for Education needs field marshals for their upcoming fundraising run. Even if none of those volunteer opportunities float your boat, just surf the (non porn) web to find something that appeals to you. Volunteering can give you a sense of purpose, expand your friend and business contact networks and just get your butt off the couch and out of the house for a few hours. Your spouse will thank you and me.

Music Playlists – If you're a man over fifty, and you have an iTunes, Spotify or Pandora account, listen to whatever the hell you want. There, I said it. Music is so subjective and should be left to one's individual taste. I, myself, still like the classic rock of Def Leppard, Fleetwood Mac and Journey along with the more timely stylings of a John Mayer, Keith Urban and Michael Franti. Now, unlike most of my Tri Valley suburban dad peers, I can also appreciate newer artists such as Childish Gambino, Post Malone and Halsey (who most of you have never heard of), along with the more pop stylings of Ed Sheeran, Bruno Mars or Florence and the Machine (who I hope some of you have heard of). Music has no age boundaries and should be appreciated as art. Now, concerts are something else completely; as I much prefer the intimate confines of a club or small venue to the craziness of an arena or amphitheater show. Call me old, but you couldn't pay me enough Bitcoin to attend Outside Lands, Snow Globe or Bottle Rock. I can only imagine what a s*#t show the three-day Coachella Music Festival would be when jostling with 250,000 people for a place to stand and watch one of the thirty acts daily. No thank you I say!

Being the music aficionado I am, I love music trivia. Did you know that more songs have been written about Saturdays than any other day of the week? You've undoubtedly heard "Saturday in the Park" by Chicago, "Saturday Night's Alright (For Fighting)" by Sir Elton John and "S-A-T-U-R-D-A-Y" by the Bay City Rollers. These are rowdy, whoop it up anthems primed for going out and having a good time. Guess what day comes in second? Mondays, probably because Mondays are the opposite of Saturdays, drab and depressing. Songs such as "I Don't Like Mondays" by The Boomtown Rates, "Manic Monday" by The Bangles, "Rainy Days and Mondays" by The Carpenters and "Monday, Monday" by The Mamas & The Papas are all pretty sad and depressing. There are songs written and recorded about every day of the week including "Ruby Tuesday," "Waiting for Wednesday" and "Thursday's Child," but Fridays and Sundays get more than their share of airplay with songs such as "Last Friday Night," "Friday I'm in Love," and "Friday on my Mind," to go along with "Sunday Bloody Sunday," "Sunday Papers" and "Sunday Morning." You might ask yourself, why is he sharing this with me? No reason, just filler to get me to my word count. I'm full of shenanigans.

Shenanigans – If you're a man over fifty, a certain amount of shenanigans should be part of your summer. There, I said it. I'm not saying "cop-calling" shenanigans, but don't' be afraid to cut loose and have a little fun from time to time. A few ideas include seeing live comedy at Tommy T's instead of another movie at the local megaplex, enjoying a game night with friends or renting the movie *Game Night*. You don't even need little ones to enjoy a romantic overnight campout. Make it a goal to attend one of the free concerts playing almost every weekend somewhere along the I-680 corridor Before the summer ends, walk barefoot on freshly cut lawn, wash your car shirtless or invite your neighbor over for a margarita and game of doorbell ditch. For gosh sakes, enjoy your summer like you did when you were young.

    I would like to thank you all for struggling with me through this year's version of my annual writer's block dribble. If my words provided you with just a small pleasant distraction to your otherwise busy and stressful day then I have done my job, which really isn't a job at all. It's more like a hobby or craft project for my scrapbook. There, I said it. Suffice it to say, how do you like those shenanigans?

12 It's My Birthday

July 29th is my birthday. Please don't buy me anything... expensive. Truth be told, I don't expect a big fuss for my birthday anymore. However, I do truly enjoy the "Likes" and "Comments" made on Facebook throughout the day, thank you Mark Zuckerberg. Since my birthday falls on a Friday this year, I'll likely go to work. It is always appreciated if someone takes me to lunch (hint, hint). We'll probably celebrate with a family dinner at Hana Japan in Dublin, since that awesome restaurant always comps the birthday boy or girl's meal. My wife will likely bake me a carrot cake because that's my favorite. My daughters make cards for me because I refuse to have anyone in my house pay for overpriced Hallmark greeting cards. The night usually concludes with me actually getting to choose what we watch on TV. A birthday is a good day.

July seems to be a very popular birthday month, given the number of friends and family who will be celebrating their birthdays this month along with me. My daughter, Claire, was born on July 6th. Our neighbor, Katie, was born on the same day at the same hospital several hours apart. My wife's Uncle Leo was also born on the 6th. My sister, Christine, was born on the 12th. My brother-in-law, Ben, celebrates his birthday on the 14th along with my great-niece Nadia, my former college roommate Jerry and my former college football coach, Jim Fairchild. Our close friend, Rhonda, is 12 days older than me (July 17), but I look much older. My good buddy Craig's BD is on the 30th. Somehow, I remember that three former girlfriends (Gloria, Stacy and Carolyn) celebrate birthdays in July (24th, 27th and the 28th), but don't tell my wife that I brought that up. I'm also expecting another great niece sometime this month.

There are several notable celebrities (past and present) who claim July as their month of birth beginning with Princess Diana (7/1). She is followed by gifted child actress Lindsey Lohan (7/2), Scientologist Tom Cruise (7/3), First Daughter Malia Obama (7/4), Jersey Shore DJ Pauly DelVecchio (7/5), former President of the United States George W. Bush (7/6), Beatles drummer Ringo Star (7/7), Six Degrees of Kevin Bacon subject Kevin Bacon (7/8), Academy Award winning actor/producer Tom Hanks (7/9), the object of my desire Sofia Vergara (7/10), rapper Lil Kim (7/11), WWE wrestler Brock Lesner (7/12), Millennium Falcon pilot, Han Solo, a.k.a. Harrison Ford (7/13), MMA Fighter Conor McGregor (7/14), comedian Gabriel "Fluffy" Inglesias (7/15), SNL funnyman - Will Ferrell (7/16), country singer Luke Bryan (7/17), Fast & Furious mastermind Vin Diesel (7/18), Bay Area cutie Riley Curry (7/19), Super model Gisele Bundchen (7/20), Mrs. Doubtfire Robin Williams (7/21), singer/actress Selena Gomez (7/22), Harry Potter Daniel Ratcliffe (7/23), entertainer extraordinaire - Jennifer "J. Lo" Lopez (7/24), football All-Pro Walter Payton (7/25), my favorite actress, Sandra Bullock and Rolling Stone Mick Jagger (7/26), Baseball player/steroid abuser A. Rod (7/27), Former First Lady, Jacqueline Kennedy Onassis (7/28), Rush bassist Geddy Lee (7/29), body builder, Arnold Schwarzenegger (7/30) and Shark Tank entrepreneur, Mark Cuban (7/31). I don't want to brag, but that's a pretty impressive line-up of like-minded individuals blowing out candles the same month as me.

If you were born in the month of July, your astrological sign is either Cancer (up to July 22nd) or Leo (7/23 forward). Thanks to www.zodiac.com, the characteristics of a Cancer and Leo are described as follows.

Cancer is a mysterious sign, filled with contradictions. The crab is Cancer's ruling animal and it suits Cancers well, they can come out of their shell and fight but they can also hide in their shell skittering away back into the depths of the ocean. They are very unpredictable. With cancer, there is always something more than meets the eye, for they are always partially hidden behind the shell. A Cancer wants security and comfort, yet seeks new adventure. They are very helpful to others yet sometimes can be cranky and indifferent. Cancer has a driving, forceful personality that can be easily hidden beneath a calm, and cool exterior. They have a deep psyche and intuitive mind that is hidden from the world. Cancers are deeply sensitive and easily hurt , this might be why they have their defense shell in place, to avoid being hurt by others. They are nurturers so they surround themselves with people, whom after a while can offend or hurt a cancer without even knowing they did so, therefore Cancer's protective shell keeps them safe from hurt. They are complex, fragile, unpredictable and temperamental and need constant support and encouragement, more than any other astrology sign, Cancer needs to be needed. When cancer gets the support it needs, it has a tremendous amount to offer in return. When cancer gets offended, they tend to sulk instead of confronting the persons face to face. This needlessly prolongs the pain and suffering. Cancer is very possessive, not just with material possessions but with people as well. Cancer will always want to stay in touch with old friends and anyone who has ever been close to them, because it is easier to maintain a friendship then attempt to learn to trust a new person. It is easier this way for them emotionally. If you befriend a Cancer, you will stay friends for a long time. Cancer makes the perfect mother, and in fact this is the sign that represents motherhood. They have unconditional love and caring more so then any other astrology sign. Cancers are very intuitive. Most of the psychics of the world are Cancer astrology signs. They have an excellent memory and are very observant and can read people very well. With their strong intuition, sensitivity, powers of observation and intelligence, Cancers will have great success in anything they undertake.

Leo is the lion, this well suited symbol represents Leo very well. They possess a kingdom which they protect and cherish. The kingdom could be anything from work to home to a partner. Leos are high esteemed, honorable and very devoted to the ones they care about. Leo is always center stage and full of flair, they enjoy basking in the spotlight. A Leo always makes their presence known. Leos are full of energy that acts like a magnet for other people. Others are attracted to Leo's wit, charm, and what they have to say for they speak of things grand and very interesting. Leo will never settle for second best and will work hard to achieve the best results. Public image is very important to Leo, with luxurious possessions and ways of life; this keeps the public image in high standing. They will do whatever it takes to protect their own reputation. People are attracted to Leo's zest for life and their warm spirit. They have the ability to lift up one's spirits and provide encouragement when times are rough. Their enthusiasm attracts people, Leos are social butterflies, not because they want to be but because people always naturally gravitate and surround the Leo. Leos are very difficult people to not like. Leos are very generous, kind and open-hearted people. If a Leo is crossed, they will strike back with force but they are not one to hold a grudge, they easily forgive, forget and move on. Leos are always trying to make things right in the world, they have larger than life emotions and they need to feel like they have accomplished something at the end of the day. They react to situations with action instead of sitting back and thinking about it, they are not impulsive however because they look at the future and consider consequences of their actions. Leos are extremely sensitive but they hide that very well. Leos love praise and flattery; their egos demand respect and adoration. Leo is all about pride. That's so me.

There was a time when I was younger that I wanted to get a tattoo of a mighty lion across my back or chest to signify strength and courage. But, by the time I turned twelve, it seemed a bit extreme. I eventually settled for a tattoo of Simba, from Disney's *The Lion King*, on my left butt cheek. It's an adorable likeness of the animated lion cub. Maybe one day I'll add Timon and Pumbaa to the other cheek.

July 4th is commonly referred to as the birthday of our nation, the good ole United States of America. Perhaps you've heard of it? Our annual birthday party for the country is a thing of beauty complete with celebrations, parades, concerts, 5K/10K fun-runs, hot dog eating contests, pool activities, egg tosses and fireworks. I love me some fireworks. That's the kind of birthday a man can only dream of, but dream I do. Happy birthday to me!

13 Mika's Houseboat Ark

As I keyboard away on my monthly piece for *ALIVE*, I might be overstating the obvious when I report that it's been raining a lot. For days and days, there has been an abundance of precipitation in our ecosystem. It makes one wonder if it will ever stop? In fact, it reminds me of that story about a man who, at the request of God, built a really big boat and stocked it with a bunch of animals before hitting the high seas for a joyous family cruise. You know the one I'm referring to, "Mika's Ark." Please allow me to tell the tale.

Their once lived a ruggedly handsome/athletically built, yet humble man who we'll call Mika (the Hebrew name for Michael or one who is like God—really). By day, Mika was a moderately successful commercial real estate agent, but at night he spread the good word. By good word I mean he wrote a monthly magazine column consisting of sophomoric humor and occasionally funny observations on life. This story is full of undeniable similarities. One day, while completely sober because it was still early, he heard a voice. The voice provided Mika with a long-term weather report and instructions on building an Ark. The voice, presumed to be God and not Al Roker, didn't take into account that Mika wasn't very skilled when it came to hammering nails or sawing wood stuff. Consequently, Mika chose to honor this divine intervention by visiting a houseboat showroom and placing an order for the biggest, baddest boat in the company's inventory.

For the houseboat aficionados in the audience, both of you, the majestic Titan is one of the grandest models in the entire houseboat fleet. This triple deck, sixty-five-foot vessel offers the finest in comfort and entertainment. A widescreen TV, home theater system with surround sound, tracking satellite, fireplace and full wet bar with a temperature-controlled wine cabinet are integrated in the main salon. Relax in the sunken hot tub or take an exhilarating ride down the enclosed spiral tube waterslide, both located on this spectacular sky deck. The Titan boasts eight HD flat screen TVs and 4 refrigerators! Sixteen people, and/or some animals, can be served at the spacious dinette, and the couches convert into 2 full sized beds. The main deck also has four private staterooms and two full baths. A sliding glass door on the starboard side of the vessel provides convenient access to and from your small boat or dock. The second story, created to offer privacy and space, provides one private stateroom and one master suite with its own entertainment system, coffee maker, fridge, microwave and private deck area. The bunkroom will accommodate six people in two double and two single bunks. For convenience, an additional full bath is on the second deck. The aft observation counter is an ideal spot for dining, relaxing and taking in the view. Located on the Titan's third deck is a designer wet bar with a fridge, propane barbecue, TV, crow's nest dining area and another aft observation counter. Obviously, some modifications will be made for the animals.

According to Genesis—the Book, not the awesome '80s rock band featuring Phil Collins, Mike Rutherford and Tony Banks—God gave Mika a blueprint for building the ark. It is presumed that God also gave Mike a Home Depot gift card because ark building ain't cheap. Given that Mika strategically choose to purchase the Titan ark instead of building one, he used the gift card for a top of the line BBQ, a really cool riding mower, an assortment of Ralph Lauren paints and a lot of doggie doors.

Seven days before the deluge, God told Mika to enter the ark with his household (family) and pairs of animals. With that, Mika and his daughters started rounding up neighborhood pets such as dogs, cats, rabbits, hamsters, guinea pigs and roaming bands of Mt. Diablo wild turkeys. Pets were easy enough to come by, but the tigers, gorillas and anacondas were a little tougher to find in the suburbs. Ultimately, he found a three-legged coyote, a blind skunk and couple of squirrels and called it a day. Fortunately, he was able to pack, excuse me, load a few extra cows and chickens just in case the kids got tired of fish, veggies and gummy bears.

As most people know, the rains lasted 40 days and 40 nights and the ark was afloat for a total of 150 days before coming to rest on the top of Mt. Diablo upon the eventual receding of the waters. Once everyone did eventually disembark, Mika grabbed a latte at Peet's Coffee & Tea and life resumed, just somewhat soggier. It is written that God caused the flood because he saw great wickedness in the people of Danville and Alamo. No big surprise there, however rumor has it that Mika did ask a few of his friends and neighbors to join he and his family on the house-boat ark, but most people thought he was seventy-two-hour hold candidate at the Contra Costa County Psych Ward or a 5150, police code for "crazy."

When it comes to movies about Noah's Ark (Noah being Mika's 2nd cousin once removed by a divorce), there's *Noah*, starring Russell Crowe, which was released in 2014, and *Evan Almighty*, starring Steve Carell released in 2007. Both have an interesting take on the whole Ark controversy and Mika appreciated each film for it's artistic beauty. At the risk of being a "buzzkill," technically, there is no scientific evidence for a global flood, and despite many expeditions, no evidence of the ark has been found. The challenges associated with housing all living animal types would have made building the ark a practical impossibility.

It won't be until the spring that we know how much rain we got this year, however, given how the year has started out we may be looking to the heavens to account for this deluge. In the meantime, you might want to consider purchasing a little dingy on Amazon or looking into a used Master Craft through Craig's List.

14 Everyone Has a Book in Them

It's been said that everyone has a book in them. Not literally, of course; that would be grossly uncomfortable. Suffice it to say that we're all filled with stories or life experiences that could or should be translated into book form. Take me, for instance. Many years before the international acclaim of my first book, *Alive and Kickin' – Sideways Views from an Upright Guy*, my wife had convinced me to record some of the bedtime stories I had been telling our two daughters on a nightly basis. These stories were made up whimsical tales utilizing characters they were familiar with such as friends, relatives, pets or dolls and stuffed animals from their rooms. It was a challenge to create nightly adventures that would gently hold their interest while often times trying to weave in some type of life lesson. I don't proclaim to be Barbara Park (Junie B. Jones series), Laura Numeroff (*If You Give a Pig a Pancake*) or Ian Falconer (Olivia the Pig series), but Hannah and Claire seemed to enjoy my stories as they drifted off to sleep.

The point is, once I purged them onto the computer, I never did anything with these brilliantly crafted pieces of my soul, until now. With the help of Eric Johnson at Alive Book Publishing, I plan to put together a book entitled, *Would Someone Please Tell Me a Story*, a collection of bedtime stories from a real-life dad. I may never sell one copy, but I'll be able to leave the book to my daughters hoping one day they'll read our stories to their children/my grandchildren just in case I'm not around to do it myself. Don't feel embarrassed if you're starting to tear up as you read this article, I have a tendency to tap into people's emotions pretty easily.

A Trip to the Big City
In a quaint little house in the suburbs, there lived two sisters,

Carly and Libby. Carly was ten years old and Libby, eight. The sisters loved to play together, read books to each other and go to the movies. Cary and Libby also liked their visits to the big city. Once every three or four months, Carly, Libby and their parents, take a forty-five-minute drive to the big city to shop, see shows, eat at new restaurants and explore the various districts that make up the metropolis. Mom and Dad call it cultural, but Carly and Libby just call it fun.

For their visits to the big city, the girls always dress nicely, do their hair and they each are allowed to bring one doll. Their favorite thing to do in the big city is to walk the busy streets. They love to buy inexpensive jewelry from the street vendors; they feed the pigeons in the park and they meet interesting people everywhere they go.

On one recent trip to the big city, Carly and her mother were sitting at an outdoor café while Libby and their father were inside ordering lunch. Off in the distance, Carly noticed a young girl about her age, sitting with an elderly woman on a bench across the plaza. Carly smiled at the girl and although the girl looked sad, she did smile back. Carly noticed that the girl had worn and ragged clothes, smudges of dirt on her cheeks and her shoes were almost worn out. Carly asked her mother why the girl looked so unhappy. When Libby and their father joined Carly and their mom for lunch, the girl's parents explained that some people in the city were homeless. Carly and Libby were unaware that some kids didn't have homes to live in, food to eat or nice clothes to wear. They both felt very lucky and at the same time compassionate for the other children.

Carly asked her parents if she could walk over and talk with the little girl on the bench. Her parents said yes and kept a close eye on her as she walked across the plaza. Carly introduced herself and gave her doll to the girl. The girl was so surprised she started to cry. The elderly woman, the girl's grandmother, told

Carly her granddaughter never had a doll. Carly had a warm feeling in her heart knowing she had done something special. When she returned to Libby and her parents, she explained what had transpired. Her parents were very proud of their daughter. Later that day, Libby gave her doll to a baby in a stroller.

From that point forward, whenever the family went to the big city, the girls always brought a toy, stuffed animal, sweater or jacket and some food to give to one of the homeless families. The girls loved their trips to the big city.

Moo, I'll Take Care of You

On a big farm, in the middle of California's Central Valley, there lived a big, beautiful Jersey milking cow named Kaye. Over the years, Kaye had birthed a great many calves all of whom had grown up to be fine cows. As Kaye grew older, she missed taking care of little ones so she started mothering any stray animal that found their way to her farm.

One cloudy day, a baby duck showed up on the farm. The duckling had become separated from her flock and was all alone on the farm. Kaye watched as the duckling wandered around the barnyard for a few days trying to find someplace to fit in until Kaye moseyed over to say hello. The little yellow-feathered bird looked up at the enormous bovine and said the only thing that came to mind: "quack." Kaye gave the adorable little quacker a sniff, smiled and responded simply by saying, "Moo, I'll take care of you," and from that day forward Kaye watched over the duck as if she was one of her very own calves. She rustled up grain for the fowl to eat, gathered loose down feathers to build a bed and learned all types of duck games to play. Kaye was the only mother the duck ever knew or needed.

Several years later, a gray and white tabby kitten showed up on the farm scared and lonely. None of the other barn animals knew where the kitten had come from or what had become of its mother. Kaye could see that the kitten's coat needed cleaning and in one lick of her enormous tongue the kitten was clean and shiny. As the kitten purred with delight, Kaye sniffed the little ball of fur and said, "Moo, I'll take care of you." Kaye found the kitten milk to drink, yarn to chase and a warm safe place to sleep. Kaye was a perfect mother to the baby cat.

Life on farm was good; however, there were never any children at the farm until one day when the farmer and his wife brought home a little girl about four or five years old. Kaye kept a watchful eye on the adventurous newcomer to the farm whenever she ventured outside to play or explore. Ultimately, the toddler found Kaye or Kaye found the toddler. Regardless, Kaye nuzzled the freckled face mop top and thought, "Moo, I'll take care of you." The farmer and his wife were wonderful parents and they raised an exceptional girl, but Kaye liked to think she helped too. Sadly, Kaye passed on several years after the girl left for college. Once the farmer's daughter became a woman, she married and had a child of her own. Not surprisingly, the new mother's first instinct was to look deeply into her baby's eyes and say, "Moo, I'll take care of you."

The Zoo

Hannah and Claire loved to visit the zoo, it was their favorite of many things they could do.

It had been a few months since their last big zoo trip, but they remembered one monkey who loved to do flips.

So Hannah asked Mom and Claire talked to Dad, they begged and they pleaded, it sounded so sad.

Yet having nice parents, who enjoyed a good time, Mom and Dad liked their idea, said it sounded just fine.

So early that Sunday, they loaded the car, they sang silly songs though it wasn't real far.

Once they arrived for their day full of fun, the girls spotted some hippos enjoying the sun.

The lions they roared and the camels were snacking, joeys in pouches kangaroos moms were packing.

Claire talked to zebras and Hannah to bears, mom whistled to parrots while dad stood and stared.

The girls laughed super loud seeing a monkey wear pants and they were truly amazed not knowing a brown bear could dance.

At the end of the day, as they all headed home, Claire wore on her head antlers made of soft foam.

Hannah sported a trunk that hung from her nose and once in the car their eyes started to close.

Mom said to Dad, "Our girls sure love the zoo." Dad just nodded his head and responded, "Yeah, they sure do!"

If you have ever considered writing a book, there is no better time than the present. It doesn't have to be the next self-help bestseller or epic novel, but it can be a piece of you to share and leave behind. Let Eric Johnson and his staff at Alive Book Publishing help you check off that next bucket list item.

ALIVE is a local publishing company enabled with the tools and expertise to effectively position, market and advertise your book using a vast array of media. While the basic essentials of book publishing are certainly important, they comprise just one dimension of what they do as part of ALIVE Media. Their publishing foundation is based upon something quite different from that of other book publishers. Their experience is based upon not only books, but eight years' experience publishing a monthly lifestyle magazine. They know what it takes to market and actually *sell* editorial products because they've been doing it successfully, every month for over eight years. When it comes to marketing, public relations and advertising, they're not "middle men," like most publishers—they actually own the tools of production and have the hands-on experience required to create and conduct a successful public relations and marketing campaign for your book.

I will be forever grateful for Eric's help and guidance. If you're currently reading this, in what is my third book with ALIVE, consider yourself one of the fortunate few. Probably very few because it's not like I'm Dave Barry (my idol). That said, I'll always be extremely proud that I was able to publish three compilation books of my articles over the past fifteen years.

15 It's a Dog's Life

I recently saw the movie *A Dog's Purpose*. It follows a dog as he is reincarnated as different breeds belonging to various owners. Over the course of several lifetimes, the dog's existence intersects with that of a young boy who rescued him in 1962. Yes, it did make me cry, but that's not the point. The thought of dog reincarnation got me to thinking. What if a human was reincarnated as a dog? Could we live that life and be content? Given the dogs I know, I'm pretty sure a dog's life would be just fine by me.

We are a two-dog household. Trudy is a thirteen-year-old Terrier mix and Molly, soon to be five, is a Rhodesian Ridgeback. For those of you unfamiliar with dogs, they are a carnivorous domesticated mammal, also known as a canine, pooch, hound, or mutt. Trudy spends most of her time napping and Molly, being more active, spends her days running around the back yard barking at birds, the wind, squirrels, undetectable sounds or the subtle shift of the earth's axis. She eats everything she encounters (i.e.; dried animal poop, dead lizards and discarded Kleenex), in addition to some gross stuff. In Dogville, life is pretty much a revolving cycle of eat, drink, lick, poop, sleep, repeat. That is the life. The closest resemblance to a dog's life that we humans can relate to is probably that of a rock star. I bet Justin Bieber, Beyonce, Lady Gaga and Pit Bull (see what I did there?) all spend their days much like Molly when they're not in the studio or on the road touring.

If I was reincarnated as a dog, I could scratch myself, clean myself, pee and poop wherever I wanted, drink from the toilet, sniff human crotches, sniff my friend's behinds (it's like shaking hands), bark/howl/growl until my throat hurt and sleep, sleep, sleep. Did I also mention that dogs don't get married? That's right, they "hook up." I don't judge them. In fact, I appreciate their animalistic approach to relationships. They take care of their primal instinct/physical urges and yet don't feel the need to comply with the institution of marriage. That's not to say that if I were a dog I would forgo my fatherly duties. I would undoubtedly want to be there for the delivery of my litter and would stick around to help raise my pups, but that whole marriage thing just isn't part of dog's life. In this dog fantasy world, I would have a neighborhood full of female "dog friends with benefits." That is until my owners took the responsible action of having me neutered. Oh, the shame. Come to think of it, once that happened, I would probably settle down with a nice collie.

If I was a dog, I would like to be a German Shepherd. Not because I'm of German decent. If human heritage was the determining factor in breed, I would be an Irish Setter/English Bulldog half-breed. German Shepherds are by nature, protective, strong, brave and intelligent. All of those qualities are admirable if you're describing a dog or fraternity brother. Growing up, my family had a pure white German Shepherd we named Snowy. I have so many good memories of times spent with that dog. Summer sleep outs in the back yard, playing fetch (him not me) at the park and long walks where we would talk about girls, baseball and girls. Snowy was deep, yet simplistic. He assessed everything he came into contact with as Friend, Foe or Food. I try and do the same in my line of work as a writer. Food is pretty easy to identify, however friend or foe can be tricky sometimes.

History is filled with famous dogs in every form of art, athletics and literature. The painting of dogs playing poker is a masterpiece. While dog fighting makes me sick, dog racing has been around since early Egyptian times. Racing the incredibly fast and agile Greyhounds is immensely popular while watching dachshunds (aka wiener dogs) is just delightfully amusing. Since 1974, there have been 62 movies, grossing over $2 billion dollars, with a dog as the central character. Dog actors, such as Lassie, Old Yeller, Rin Tin Tin, Toto, Benji, Air Bud and the Shaggy D.A. haven't won any Academy Awards (yet), but they have made significant contributions to some wonderful movies. There have been dogs on television going back fifty years, starting with Pete, Spanky's Pit Bull on *Little Rascals*, Tiger, a sheep dog who lived with the Brady Bunch, Buck, also a sheep dog who housed with the Bundys on *Married with Children* and finally Eddie, the cute little Jack Russell terrier on *Frasier*. Many of us can all recall commercial pitch dogs like Loren Green's dog, Duke, chasing sticks for Alpo as well as The Taco Bell Chihuahua and Budweiser's Spuds Mackenzie. There are also the always entertaining comic strip and cartoon dogs including Marmaduke, Scooby Doo, Under Dog, Lady and the Tramp, Clifford, the big red dog, Bolt and, of course, Snoopy. Finally, in literature, who could forget Shiloh, White Fang or Cujo? However, to truly understand dogs, take the time to read the beautifully crafted book, *The Art of Racing in the Rain* by Garth Stein. The story is told in the words/thoughts of Enzo, a Golden Retriever. If you ever wondered what a dog was thinking, this book provides you with an enlightening notion.

I'm not saying everything about a dog's life is ideal. Dogs can't get a job, pay bills, drive carpool, vote, invest for retirement, clean the house, "Tweet", shop, mow the lawn or dance. Who am I kidding? I don't like to do any of those things. Dogs don't need materialistic possessions or stressful responsibilities. Sure, they might bark from time to time, but that's just to be heard and acknowledged. Similar to when I raise my voice (aka bark). Given the possibility of reincarnation, maybe I should request to be a dog in my next life. Years from now, hopefully many years from now, I could see myself as a happy little mutt living with a nice family in the suburbs. My name might be Buddy or Champ and I'll wag my tail, sit and even learn how to shake my paw. If someone will occasionally throw me a Frisbee and rub my belly this dog's life would be good.

Sidebar: If you're considering adding a dog to your family, visiting the local area animal shelters in hopes of finding a compatible canine is actually quite enjoyable. We found Trudy at the SPCA in Dublin. The SPCA has a beautiful facility, qualified staff, educational classes and a very nice collection of mature adult dogs. Our area also supports other organizations such as ARF and East Bay Animal Shelter. Adopted dogs are wonderful in large part due to their appreciative attitude having been given a second lease (or leash) on life. I suppose knowing that if you aren't adopted you may be chasing Frisbees in heaven makes rescue dogs inherently grateful.

16 It's Tough to be a Kid Today

I don't think I would make it as a kid today. For starters, I'm terrible at video games. Unless I'm mistaken, the only way to be accepted by a middle school pack of boys is to be a proficient gamer. There are a plethora of other challenges that the kids (more specifically boys) contend with daily, which leads me to believe that most of us who grew up in the '70s and '80s couldn't hack it in today's world. My guess is virtually all of us would crumble like a high protein energy bar if we were to somehow spend time as a middle school student today with a junior high school student mentality or frame of reference from yester-year.

My Isaac Newton Graham Junior High School days were filled with school, friends, sports, girls/hormones, TV, family and my neighborhood. I lived a typical suburban life similar to the one described in Steve Rushin's book *Sting-Ray Afternoons*. My unofficial book review rates this a must-read for anyone fifty to sixty years of age.

School is a lot tougher than it used to be. There's more pressure than ever to deliver good grades and establish good study habits straight out of elementary school. Most of my buddies and I pretty much skated through the seventh and eigthth grade on our wit and good looks. We all thought you didn't really need to apply yourself until high school. Nowadays, you would think your kid's middle school grades are part of their UC college admission application. "Sorry Mike, you're just not UCLA material due to that C you got in seventh grade woodshop class." Candidly, I was never UCLA material.

Grant H, 8th Grade Los Ceros Middle School: "There's a lot of pressure to do good in school and it's tough juggling school with sports and everything else. There's always a lot of work to stay up on and you can't afford to get behind if you want to maintain good grades."

Kevin A. 8th grader at Harvest Park Middle School: "School puts a lot of pressure on all of us. It's not just from parents and teachers. There's a lot of competition with friends at school. Everybody wants to do well at school, sports and everything to prepare for high school."

In our day, it was the jocks and cheerleaders who ran the school, but today, it's science & mathaletes who call the shots. Future app developers and start-up entrepreneurs control the lunchroom power as they offer stock options for early VC funding.

Sports: Dressing for PE was mandatory in the '70s and it didn't take long to figure out who the alpha males were based on their size, speed and skill set. Guys like Russell Peoples, Frank Dowse, Ron Mendez, Mike Lara were feared and revered due to their superior athletic abilities. PE class, after school sports and neighborhood pick-up games taught us the importance of teamwork, communication, time management and conflict resolution. It seems today that boys are either over committed with overlapping team activities or they can opt out of sports for any variety of reasons including anxiety, stress or having an allergic reaction to Axe body spray. A lot of tween-age boys idea of exercise in 2019 is playing Fortnite online.

Reilly G., 8th Grade at Charlotte Wood Middle School: "There's always pressure at school because we have so much going on after school. I often feel overworked and tired because I go from one thing to another without a lot of down time."

Friends are often our lifeline during the turbulent times of adolescence. Keeping in mind that my middle school years took place shortly after the very first video game (Pong) was released, unlike today's youth, my gang of hooligans didn't let it take over our lives. Jeff, Derek, Mark, Luis and I chose to occupy our after school and weekend hours with an assortment of neighborhood games (tag, hide and seek and door bell ditch) along with riding our bikes. "Be home by dark" was my mom's go-to line as I headed out the door. I liked that line much better than "Just wait until your father gets home." I had a paper route with the San Jose Mercury News to make a little spending money. Kids today probably don't know what a newspaper is let alone the notion of folding, packing and throwing them at houses from a moving bicycle. Do kids even ride bicycles anymore or do they rely on Uber to get them everywhere even if it's just a few blocks away? A bike used to mean freedom and independence. That said, my Uber driver's name was "Mom" and she always helped me deliver my newspapers on rainy days.

Cooper P. 8th grader at St. Isidore School: "I love the time away from school when I get to work out in the gym. The more you put into it the more the more you get out of it. The trainers at Cal Strength really help you to learn the proper techniques to help you reach your goals."

Girls or just an attraction to someone of the opposite sex (or same sex) is a confusing stage at any age, but in those early teen years it can be downright petrifying. Who of us understood what we were feeling or thinking, let alone the reactions our body was processing during that turbulent time of puberty? My harmless early crushes included Pam, Linda, Judy, Elise and Kristy among others. They don't even make names like those anymore. It's a shame that I couldn't bottle and sell nervous perspiration because I had plenty of that coursing over my body anytime one of those young ladies crossed by path near a locker, in the lunch line or siting next to me in a class. Thank goodness for school dances and Forget Me Not fundraisers.

Our pre-disco era school dances were held on Friday nights and hosted live bands covering the most popular songs of The Eagles, Fleetwood Mac and Steely Dan. This was the best time to talk, flirt and interact with someone you were smitten by, but couldn't muster the courage to approach during the typical school day. A Forget Me Not fundraiser allowed kids to send flowers or candy to someone during sixth period, usually around a holiday like Halloween, Christmas or Valentine's Day. Thankfully, we could also send an anonymous FMN to a special friend we might be "crushing" on. Even though none of the girls mentioned above were ever interested in me, they probably all received a carnation or candy cane from me with a note signed "Your Secret Admirer." Today, that would be grounds for expulsion for expressing unwanted attention, but back then it was just sweet.

Hannah O., 8th grader at St. Isidore School. "Some boys are really immature and some are nice and polite. Our school doesn't allow use to use phones on campus so it kind of forces us to talk to each other more, but all of the boys are obsessed with video games and that's all they ever talk about."

Television is obsolete. Despite having hundreds of mainstream and cable channels to select from, most kids don't seem to have time for television. As a kid, I spent way too many hours in front of a TV. I don't want to brag, but we had two TVs in our house, one color and one black & white. Today, on the rare occasion when kids do have down time, they stream Netflix on their computer or phone in the privacy of their bedrooms. Our TV viewing was always in the family room, usually with Mom and Dad as company. Programs such as *MASH, Good Times* and

Happy Days have been replaced by the likes of *Stranger Things, The Walking Dead* and *Ridiculousness*. I would gladly trade being the human remote for a little me time.

Social Media: Since texting has replaced talking, I would first need to become immersed in social media for all my communication needs. Every middle schooler today seems to have an Apple iPhone 10X, Apple Watch and wireless Apple ear buds and I'm barely able to operate my two-year-old iPhone 6 without having to ask my teenage daughter how to insert a smiley face emoji in a text. I long for the days when my entire family shared one landline with a very long extension cord for those private closet conversations. I've already written about the fear every teen boy had when calling a girl's house and getting her dad on the line. I still break out in a sweat thinking about Mr. Boudreau's phone interrogations and I'm older now than he was then. What type of trouble would I have gotten into with Snap Chat or Instagram, you ask? Trust me, you don't even want to know.

I get the impression that kids are under a lot of pressure these days. Pressure to do well in school, excel in sports or other extracurricular activities and even social media pressure. I'm sure we had pressures too although for the life of me I can't remember what they might have been. I think of the wasted days and fun filled nights that we had and I feel bad that kids today don't know what it's like to have that type of freedom. It's a different time and I get the impression it's much tougher to be a kid today.

17 Dan Donnelly
College Football's Tailgating Entrepreneur

Dan Donnelly loves college football. He loves the collegiate school spirit, the pageantry, the rivalries, the marching bands and the buzz around campus leading up to a Saturday afternoon kickoff. He loves rankings and bowl match-ups, cheer squads and mascots, but he especially loves a good tailgate. His passion and enthusiasm were infectious when I talked with him over a cup of coffee one morning in late July. As the founder of Tailgate Connect, Dan is setting out to connect like-minded people in parking lots across America to share food and drink, stories, and traditions in an all-inclusive hassle-free tailgating environment through his innovative website. You had me at football, Dan. Sign me up!

Originally from Rockville, Maryland, Dan (55) played college rugby at Frostburg State University in Maryland, but he grew up an avid college football fan. In 2004, he set out on a quest to take in a game and tailgate party at every college FBS (Football Bowl Subdivision) and many of the major rivalries in the lower divisions. "In 2008, I created Dan from the Tailgate, a blog to document my journeys, allowing like-minded fans and folks I've met along the way to join me in celebrating the greatest game experience on earth," Dan proudly states. "Along the way, some of my best experiences was when I was introduced to a local tailgate host, usually through a mutual friend, and I got a chance to soak up the local flavor and atmosphere with passionate college football fans." I always had a great experience and have made some life-long friends," he proclaims.

Dan says it was not unusual to see groups of people, usually visiting fans, wandering aimlessly on campus carrying an open twelve-pack of beer and bag of chips, with no set pre-game destination. Dan candidly admits, "I've even been that guy more times than I care to admit." While attending the USC vs. Penn State Rose Bowl in 2017, he invited a group of "nomadic" Penn State fans he had never met to join his tailgate and the concept to connect fans with experienced tailgater hosts was born. For a reasonable cost (around forty dollars), guests can enjoy food and libations in a quality environment while gaining inside knowledge of the history and tradition of the host school, student body and alumni. Hosts, on the other hand, could defray sunk costs, meet new friends, learn a little something about the visiting team and make some easy cash by welcoming newcomers to the pre- and post-game activities.

Shortly after that Rose Bowl experience, Dan tightened up his business plan, incorporated, and with the help of Joe Rogers, VP of operations, secured domain names and submitted a trademark application. "A friend for eight years, it was Joe's idea to monetize the concept and he began the early work on the website and social media campaign," Dan says. Since then, the company has added Dan's college rugby teammate, Jim Devine, as controller and Theresa Baumgartner as Chief Legal Counsel. "Once the train left the station, we started recruiting top tier hosts from across the nation who would be interested in hosting guests," Dan says. Many of these tailgaters are well known in college football circles and have been featured on national TV or ranked in nationwide tailgate competitions. So far they have over 40 hosts signed up around the country including thirty-eight Division I and two Division II schools such as; the University of Texas, Nebraska, LSU, Michigan, Arkansas, Stanford, Georgia, Arizona, Colorado, Ole Miss, Minnesota, Tennessee, Arkansas, Penn State, Iowa State and Kentucky, to name just a few . The next step was to reach out to the actual colleges that traveled large groups of fans for away games. Dan and his team have connected with travel coordinators for Gridiron Clubs across the country knowing those group's members often like to mix with the home team crowds prior to a game.

The concept lays out something like this: a local or traveling fan planning to attend a game visits the Tailgate Connect website, plugs in the date and location and for forty dollars per guest is provided with a host contact (email and mobile phone number) along with a pinpoint locator map identifying the tailgate location. "Some of our smallest hosts (Boston College) have room for two to four guests and some of our largest hosts (University of Texas, Austin) have room for a hundred. Zero week "kicks-off" August 26th with four D1 games, however, Labor Day, is the official start to the college football season."

As a VP of Sales for a tech company, Dan travels a lot for business which affords him the ability to attend a lot of games on the road. He's been known catch two, occasionally three games, if geography and schedules cooperate. With one daughter graduated from Boise State (Rachel) and one who just graduated from the University of Oklahoma (Erin), it also allowed Dan the chance to visit his girls while still promoting the Dan from the Tailgate brand. His youngest (Grace) is now a sophomore on the Pom team at Monte Vista High School and dad has promised to work a little closer to home this upcoming season in order to see her perform at a majority of the Friday night home games. His wife, Amy, has always been a big supporter of Dan's passion and attends a couple of games a year with him.

To no surprise, Dan is commonly asked his favorite place to tailgate and watch a game. Without any hesitation, Donnelly proclaims, The Grove at Ole Miss. The Grove has been called "The Holy Grail of Tailgating." Located on the Oxford, Mississippi campus, the ten-acre site regularly attracts upwards of 100,000 of the most loyal college football fans tailgating on any given game day. Steeped in tradition and revelry, The Grove opens on Friday night and closes three hours after an exciting SEC game played in front of 64,000 people at Vaught-Hemingway stadium. Second to Ole Miss would be LSU at Tiger Stadium in Baton Rouge, LA, followed by, in no particular order, University of Oklahoma, Army, Clemson, Arkansas, Auburn and University of Washington. At last count, Dan has been to over 100 different venues and experienced over 150 tailgate events.

Using football vernacular, Dan hopes Tailgate Connect scores a touchdown this upcoming season. Dan shares, "Tailgating has become a personal space sharing experience much like Uber or Airbnb. It's an added element to just attending a game and a win-win for the host and their guests." For more information on Tailgate Connect check out their website at www.tailgateconnect.com or visit Dan's Blog at dantailgate.blogspot.com. Personally, I can't wait to experience the tailgating phenomenon through Tailgate Connect while visiting my daughters at their respective colleges or attending a local game this fall.

18 Planting My Beer Garden

I'm sitting here at the Danville Brewing Company, waiting for a few friends to arrive for a much-needed Guys Night Out (and Uber ride home), and I realized that I've written over 200 articles for *ALIVE* and not one has been about beer. This is an interesting fact because I really like beer. Truth be told, I've always liked beer, especially with pizza, but over the last couple of years I've grown to really appreciate a finely crafted brew. I'm mostly a wheat beer Hefeweizen kind of guy, but as a side effect of my mid-life crises, I'm starting to challenge my taste buds and venture out to try and enjoy an IPA, lager, pilsner, stout and pale ale. I feel so mature.

My friends are such beer snobs. They tell me they'll only drink craft brews. I said to them, "if you like Kraft beer you'll love their mac n' cheese." —Tony Camin, comedian

While recently moving our daughters out of their freshman dorm rooms at the University of Colorado, a friend and I found an inviting food and libations establishment called Murphy's Tap House in Louisville, CO. While engaged in a stimulating conversation with Matthew, the Master Brewer, we came to the realization that the brew pub has in some respects become a late afternoon/evening extension to the popular coffee establishments (Starbucks, Peet's and Tully's) as a trendy place to hang out and socialize with friends, neighbors and business associates. You need not look any further than Starbucks recent experiment adding beer on tap to their menu. Ultimately, either the idea of a wide-awake drunk or the Sumatra IPA didn't pan out. Starbucks has more recently announced an end to the pilot program.

The emergence of countless new beer emporiums is predicated on the demand from beer happy patrons anxious to experience the latest and greatest bold Belgians or Saisons. While other might prefer the hoppy greatness or dark and malty boldness of a flight or pint of ale from the states or abroad. Let's not forget the light and refreshing options or an occasional Sourhouse. If I come off as a beer aficionado, it's because I am considering becoming an uncertified beer cicerone, the equivalent of a wine sommelier.

My husband and I love visiting breweries and tap houses because they are a great place to socialize with friends and you get to try new beers. I don't think the appeal will fade out as long as the brewers don't run out of ideas/recipes and continue to brew high quality beer. —Michele Milz, Livermore.

If you're a statistics nerd, like me, you'll appreciate that the National Brewers Association (the other "NBA") reports that the U.S. consumed approximately $107.6 billion of beer last year of which $23.5 billion was craft beer. Overall craft beer consumption is up approximately 6.2% in the United States. The Home Brewers Association ("HBA") states that there are over 1.2 million home brewers in the United States. According to HBA statistics, two-thirds of the 1.2 million started brewing in 2005 or later, the average home brewer is forty years old, 78% are married or in a domestic partnership, 68% have a college degree, collectively they produce over 2 million barrels of beer annually. Geographically home brewers are spread across the country as follows; 31% in the West/23% Midwest/26% South/17% North-East Coast. For more information check out HopTech Homebrewing Supplies in Dublin.

I like the science aspect of brewing beer and the social aspect of drinking beer. —Craig Nunn, home brewer.

Beer played an integral part of my social maturation in high school, er... I mean college, once I turned twenty-one, of course. A Friday afternoon brew at the campus pub was a great way to wrap up an exhausting and stressful week of lectures, assignments, homework, essays, group projects, exams and pursuing coeds. I spent many a Sigma Chi fraternity party hanging around a keg collaborating with my brothers on the merits of abolishing pledge hazing, the importance of themed sorority mixers and the constant need to update our CSUN test and essay library. I was convinced that beer consumed responsibly and in moderation can be a great source of carbohydrates and nutrients. I don't, however, recommend it as a substitute for meals.

Sadly, my limited college budget regulated my beer choices to Hamm's, Pabst Blue Ribbon (aka "PBR") Meister Brau, Schlitz, Olympia, Miller, Keystone and Old Milwaukee. Splurging for the expensive stuff (to impress a sorority girl or her father) meant coughing up several more dollars a six-pack for the golden tastes of Lowenbrau, Molson, Fosters, St. Pauli Girl, Lone Star or the premium name at the time, Heineken. I do find it amusing that several of my high-falutin bowling buddies casually refer to a few of the above referenced brands as Satan's urine. I bet they weren't so pretentious when they were young, dumb and broke.

My introduction into a new form of "craft" beer began in the late '80s. These ales, were heavier, richer and a lot more flavorful than was my naïve palette had ever experienced. A variety of brands that included Sam Adams, Sierra Nevada, Rolling Rock. Anchor Steam, Redhook and Pete's Wicked Ale brightened my previously dull beer-drinking repertoire. In 1987, the Tied House opened in downtown Mountain View, my hometown. The brainchild of Lou Jemison and Andreas Haller, it was fashioned after a microbrewery in Andreas' hometown of Beden, Germany. It took a little while to catch on, but once it did it became, and continues to be the "o-to place for locals and visitors alike. Sometime later, Stoddard's Brewery in Sunnyvale opened, followed by Gordon Biersch in San Jose.

Today, the variety of specialty and craft beer is almost immeasurable. Visit any BevMo OR Trader Joes and your head will spin upon viewing the humongous selection. As I am always open to trying something new, recommendations and/or gifts are encouraged. Please feel free to drop off a growler or six-pack of your preferred brew at the Alive world headquarters in Alamo. Until then, I think I'll work up a plan to plant my own beer garden. Octoberfest is right around the corner.

Favorite Home Town Brewery – The Tied House, Mountain View. I drop by whenever I'm in the old neighborhood.

Favorite Brewery Visit When Traveling North on I-5, Fall River Tap House, Redding, CA. I drop by whenever I'm in the neighborhood.

Favorite Local Brewery: Danville Brewing Company – try the Poke Nachos with any beer on the menu. DBC is in my neighborhood.

Favorite Tri Valley Brewery: Altamont Beer Works, Livermore. Somewhat in the neighborhood.

Favorite Hole in the Wall Brewery: Schubros Brewery, San Ramon. Neighborhood.

Favorite Brewery Vacation Spot: Bend, Oregon. Over 27 brewpubs are sprinkled throughout the town. A bit of a drive to be in that neighborhood.

Favorite Six Pack for Parties – SOMA IPA by Tapstone Brewing Company

Favorite Beer Publication - *THIRST*, published and distributed in Colorado.

19 Our International Pub Crawl
and Travel Log

Despite the underwhelming response to the "My Beer Garden" article in the July issue of *ALIVE*, Eric Johnson, CEO of Alive World Wide, graciously bestowed upon me the enviable assignment to write an investigative journalist piece on pubs, inns and taverns throughout the United Kingdom. Who could say no to an all-expenses paid "stamps in my passport" trip to sample beers, lagers and ales (not to mention a little whiskey) from Great Britain and the Isle of Ireland? Truth be told, I drank more beer over the eight days of our tour than I did in the eight months leading up to the trip. Now my liver needs a vacation.

Saturday: Our trip began with a short plane ride from San Jose Airport to Seattle where, due to a four-and-a-half hour layover, we decided to give the magazine credit card a tryout by joining our friends, Dave and Roxanne, for lunch and a couple beers at the Roanoke Inn on Mercer Island. After relaxing on the deck on a beautiful sun filled day, it was back on a plane for an eight-and-a-half hour flight to Heathrow Airport in merry old London, England.

Sunday: Upon arrival and checking our bags at the hotel, our first sleep deprived stop (after some light shopping at Harrods) was to a wonderfully authentic Chelsea pub called Churchill Arms. Later that evening, we had another beer at the Lion & Staff followed by a satisfying classic fish n' chips dinner at Brew Masters in the Piccadilly Circus area (London's version of Times Square). Thanks to my iphone notes app, I was diligently logging in all of our stops because the memory app in my brain is forever crashing.

Monday: Bright and early, we boarded a Trafalgar coach (fancy English term for bus) and headed north into the England countryside. Upon arriving in Stratford upon Avon, birthplace of Shakespeare, we made our way to the Yard of Ales. From there we made a three-hour drive to the Golden Fleece (often seen on English TV's Most Haunted) in the town of York. I think the ghosts drank some of my beer because three pints later, I barely had a buzz. Dinner that evening was at a beautiful little establishment known as the Pine Marten Pub & Eating House in Harrogate, which also had twelve rooms available for weary visitors. Apparently, we weren't weary enough because we stayed at a fancy hotel adjacent to the Harrogate Convention Center some fifteen miles away.

Tuesday: We traveled through the Lake District of northern England and stopped in a charming lakeside town for lunch. We dined at a delightful little café across the street from a three hundred-year-old cemetery, however, my chicken-pot-pie tasted like it was three hundred years old. Later that day, as we crossed over to Scotland, we sampled some Gretna Green whiskey at the rest stop distillery. Highway rest stops are a somewhat unusual location for a whiskey distillery, but being a foreigner I wasn't judging the Scots. At sunset, we toured Stirlin Castle and the William Wallace Memorial. For dinner, we strapped on our kilts to enjoy a traditional haggis dinner at MacDonald Crutherland, a restaurant located at the base of the castle. Personally, I prefer my haggis served with secret sauce between two lightly toasted buns, like every other McDonald's meal, but it wasn't all that bad. It reminded me of a soggy meatball.

Wednesday: What a wonderful day we had touring Edinburgh, starting with another castle and ending with a cup of coffee at The Elephant House. This is where J.K. Rowling penned her moderately successful Harry Potter novel series. Perhaps you've heard of it? Prior to our mid-afternoon caffeine fix, we enjoyed lunch and a pint at the Malt Shovel, and another pint at Deacon Broadie's Tavern. It was very warm that day. There might also have been a Scotch stop somewhere in there.

I'm told that night we dined at The Corinthian Club in Glasgow, but for the life of me I don't remember it. This either means I was blacked out drunk from all the drink in Edinburgh, or I went into a food coma from the heaping helping of haggis, smoked haddock and porridge we apparently ate. I'm told that I especially liked the blood pudding for dessert. I think I had seconds.

Thursday/Friday: Perhaps the coolest bar we visited the entire trip was The Crown in Belfast, Ireland. This ornately decorated bar had so much character, so much history (established in 1848) and so many beers to choose from while we relaxed in a snug (small enclosed booth) with some of the locals. If The Crown was my favorite watering hole, Searsons of Baggot Street in Dublin, Ireland, was my favorite meal. I had a lamb shank and Shepherd's pie that brought me to tears. Not to mention, an Irish coffee (in Ireland) that was to die for.

Friday: On our second day in Dublin, we visited the impressive Guinness Storehouse located in the St. James's Gate Brewery district of downtown. The tour started in the Gravity Bar on the seventh floor of the massive beer distribution facility and we worked our way down to the ground floor gift shop sipping numerous pints along the way. The Guinness Storehouse is the most popular tourist destination in all of Ireland. Kiss the Blarney Stone? I was kissing the Guinness tap as we were taught how to draw the perfect pint of dark stuff.

Fortunately for us, Guinness was a short stumble to the Teeling Whiskey distillery. The Teeling Whiskey Distillery is Dublin's newest destination for whiskey fans and anyone with an interest in Dublin's long associations with Irish whiskey. Located in the heart of Dublin's City Centre, Teeling is the only operational distillery in the city.

Several dozen whiskey samples later, I swear I saw two

leprechauns making out in the parking lot. We finally stopped for a little food at the Blarney Inn just to let the fish n' chips soak up some of the alcohol. Did you know, the rock band Thin Lizzy (The Boys are Back in Town, Jailbreak, Whiskey in the Jar) was from Dublin? There is a bronze statue of the late lead singer, Phil Lynott, in the city square.

That night, we enjoyed a wonderful cabaret show at The Castle Arms, a thatched roof restaurant and playhouse. Admittedly, I do enjoy me some good Celtic riverdancing, but it was an 80-year-old comedian who brought the house down. He did a solid forty-five-minute set that killed. We ended the evening in the hotel bar singing Van Morrison songs and enjoying another Irish coffee until wee in the morn.

Saturday: We migrated south toward Waterford, Ireland, where, after storming another castle in Kilkenny, we lunched at Kyteler's Inn, established in 1450. Apparently the original proprietor was burned at the stake, presumably due to assumptions that she was a witch, although it could also have been due to incredibly slow service. Touring the Waterford Crystal factory was a lot cooler than I anticipated. Good thing I was sober when we toured the gift shop.

Dinner that night was at the lovely Saratoga (seaside) Inn where we were treated to some authentic Irish folk music performed by four old Irish guys. A geriatric version of U2, if the Edge could only remember two chords and Bono was extremely overweight and toothless (but still wearing designer shades). Our travel companion Alex proposed to his gal, Kayla, on the shore of the Irish Sea that evening. Upon returning to the hotel, we discovered that there was a street festival going on, hosted by five local clubs, and featuring a cool techno band fronted by twin sisters who were obviously the love children of Bjork and the band Devo. Given that the sun doesn't set until 10:30, this was a great way to wrap up a quick stop in Waterford.

Sunday proved to be a long day of coach and ferry travel as we crossed from Ireland to Wales. Dinner was at the scenic Llamerch Vineyard in the countryside of Pontyclun – Hensol. The wine wasn't anything to write home about, too sweet for my sophisticated palate, but the setting was beautiful and they poured a mean Fuller's lager.

Monday: Our first stop of the day was Bath, England and a delightful lunch at Sally Lunn's Buns. I believe there we enjoyed a pint of Diet Coke in our efforts to dry out a bit in anticipation of our visit to Stonehenge. Stonehenge, for those unaware, is a rock formation undoubtedly assembled by a group of inebriated aliens. It's actually very impressive given the engineering and slave labor involved if you don't buy into the extraterrestrial conspiracy.

We ultimately arrived back in London, England just in time for a final couple of pints, and another amazing lamb dinner at the Rose Pub. The Rose is located on the bank of the Thames River. After dinner, we walked past Big Ben, the Houses of Parliament and Westminster Abby enjoying a beautiful London evening on our way back to the hotel.

Tuesday was our departure day and the first day of rehab. I watched several historical movies of the countryside we had just toured during our flight home. First, *Braveheart* for Scotland; next was *Michael Collins* for Ireland; and finally, *Bridget Jones Diary* for England. All and all, our international pub crawl and tour of the United Kingdom was a wonderful experience.

This article could not have been possible without the contributions of the following people. I would first like to thank our amazing Trafalgar tour guide Gino DiLulio from Wales. Next, I would like to credit our travel companions Kim & Craig Nunn, Kyle & Emily Nunn, Kayla Nunn & Alex Johnston. Additionally, gratitude goes out to our international travel group including Craig & Jodi Miller from Bundall, Australia, The Van Der Merwe

Family from Johannesburg South Africa, Jeff Lyddon & Renita Elzinga from Ontario, Canada and George & Lillian Payne from Lusake, Zambia. Best wishes and safe travels to all on your next adventure.

20 I Am The Last Emperor
No Stamp in My Passport

At last quarter's Alive staff meeting, editor Eric Johnson encouraged us to pitch new article ideas. I jumped up and said, "Chief," (that's what I call him around the office) "what about a follow-up piece to my International Pub Crawl article that was so warmly received by the Alive readership family in the summer of 2017?" As you may recall, that popular piece chronicled my adventures traveling through England, Ireland, Scotland and Wales, visiting as many pubs as possible, complete with massive beer consumption. Trust me, it was huge! My new idea was a pub and beer tour through Eastern China. Fortunately for me, EJ loved it. He tossed me the company credit card and simply said, "Go for it, Ace." That's what he calls me around the office: Ace.

Unbeknownst to me, or Mr. Johnson apparently, I was soon to discover that China only has about five makers of beer (Tsingtao, Hans, Snow, Sunage and Yanjing) and virtually no neighborhood pubs in a country of approximately 1.4 billion people. Despite the fact that all five beers taste somewhat like a watered-down version of Pabst Blue Ribbon, someone (the Chinese government) is missing one heck of a pub franchise moneymaking opportunity given their nation's sports spectator preclusion for soccer, basketball and ping-pong.

So instead of a pub tour, I hooked up with a Citslinc Chamber of Commerce Tour. The good news is with a tour is everything is scheduled. The bad news about a tour is everything is scheduled. Upon arriving after a twelve-hour China Air flight, we stopped for the first of approximately seventeen meals consisting of Chinese food over ten days. Now I love me some tasty Chinese food from China Village in Dublin, but eating it for every lunch and dinner had me craving a peanut butter sandwich about halfway through the itinerary.

With a C of C tour, we visited a Jade Factory, Pearl Factory, Xi'an Art/Terra-Cotta Warrior Factory, Lacquer Furniture Factory, a Silk Garment Institute, The Mei Family Tea Farm in the Plum Valley and the Silk Embroidery Gallery. We were educated at each stop by charismatic spokesmen and women who all closed with first-class sales pitches as part of their presentations. Yes, you read correctly. I'm confident there is a Chinese movie equivalent to *Glengarry Glen Ross* because if "coffee (or tea in this case) is for closers," these folks were swimming in coffee/tea swimming pools because they could certainly close a sale. It was hard not to leave with something at each of the places we visited, but when will I actually wear my new silk boxer shorts embroidered with a dragon?

The two biggest cities we visited were Shanghai and Beijing. They are a lot like New York City on New Year's Eve if the Super Bowl was being played in Times Square during the Consumer Electronics Show. Better yet, imagine the population of the Top 10 U.S. cities: New York City (8,550,405), Los Angeles, (3,971,883,) Chicago, (2,720,546), Houston, (2,296,224), Philadelphia, (1,567,442,) Phoenix, (1,563,025,) San Antonio (1,469,845), San Diego, (1,394,928,) Dallas (1,300,092), and San Jose, (1,026,908) and that equals China's most populated city, Chongqing's 30,000,000 people. An unsubstantiated source (my wife) told me that half of the construction cranes in the world are in China which is not hard to believe given the massive development going on in every city we visited. The elevated freeways, skyscrapers and bridges are straight out of the movie *Blade Runner*. These cities literally never sleep as construction crews run 24/7. The most staggering products are the enormous residential condos peppering the skylines. These aren't stand-alone buildings, but five to twenty-five building campuses that stand between twenty and forty stories tall.

In addition to Beijing and Shanghai, we also stopped for a

cup of tea and a happy house (aka bathroom) break in the cities of Xi'an, Suzhou and Hangzhou. Several memorable sites throughout our tour included: the Temple of Heaven built in 1420 A.D., the Olympic Village, Tiananmen Square and the Forbidden City, the Emperor's Summer Palace, the Wild Goose Pagoda, Xi'an's Ancient City Wall, Banpo Museum/Pre-Historical Caveman Site, the West Garden Temple, cruises on the West Lake and down a portion of the Grand Canal, the Longjing Green Tea Plantation, the Pagoda of Six Harmony overlooking the Qiantang River, a ride on the Magnetic Levitation train (at 280 mph) and my two favorites, the Terra-Cotta Warriors excavation site at the Tomb of the first Emperor of the Qin Dynasty and walking on The Great Wall.

Our tour guides during our trip were Kevin, Melanie and John. Even if I could spell their Chinese names I certainly could never pronounce them. All three were engaging, highly educated and very entertaining. Not only did they tackle English as a second language, they've also managed to incorporate humor in their dialogue with us *yúchɤn dì měiguó rén* (simple Americans).

This trip would not have been as fun without the participation of the other members of my tour group including Julie Copeland, Joan and Richard Means, Randy and Emily Yim, Michael and Emma Wong, Janet and John Silva, Dennis and Rose Richardson, Karen and Dan Towel, Robert and Sally Pettit, Linda Evans and Jim Silvers, Kim Bowers and Nes Albano, Norma McTyer, Jasmen Howe, Amy Anderson, Mary Jo Della Maggiore, Joe Fontes, Judy Rice Rice and Jeanne Rogers. I also want to thank our Pleasanton Chamber of Commerce trip coordinator, the lovely and talented, Miss Kate D'Or.

My only regret is that, because I was traveling on a group visa, I did not get a stamp in my passport. Sad face emoticon because, as my new hoodie proclaims, I am the Last Emperor.

21 The Rain in Spain
An unofficial and unauthorized
international writing assignment

Virtually all, meaning none, of my loyal readers know that my oldest daughter, Hannah, is studying abroad this semester in Barcelona. That's in Spain. Being the proud opportunist that I am, I approached Eric "Chief" Johnson at Alive about the possibility of another all-expenses paid boondoggle to wrap up my travel trilogy chronicling my food and alcohol consumption in another country.

In the summer of 2017, I convinced my naïve editor that we, meaning I, should be tasked to write a European travelogue article to follow up my American beer piece. "My International Pub Crawl" highlighted suds tasting in the countries of England, Ireland, Scotland and Wales and was critically acclaimed and garnered numerous awards at the RIMAS, the Regional Independent Magazine Awards Show. I'm kind of a big deal there.

The pub crawl piece was followed up by my "I am the Last Emperor" blockbuster article chronicling my tour of China during the spring of 2018. The beer was pretty bad; however, the travels through such a majestic country were life-changing. I walked on the Great Wall, I walked the halls of the Imperial Palace and I walked the pits of the terracotta warriors along with the streets of Shanghai and Beijing. Obviously, I did a lot of walking on that trip, but that article walked me right into another big night at the RIMAs. Imagine Michael Jordon in his prime and you start to get the picture.

That leads us to my editorial staff pitch about a little wine tasting adventure in Barcelona. My angle was that while Californians have been conditioned to overpay for mediocre red, white and rosé wines just because they're from Napa, Sonoma or Pasa Robles, a lot of European wines and more specifically,

Espana wines are very affordable and mucho delicioso. That's Spanish for really good. When Chief asked to see my corporate credit card, I was assuming it was just to check the expiration date, instead he cut it in half and said, "Ace, your traveling days on the magazine's nickel are over." What a buzzkill! Knowing that I had another RIMA award in me, I decided to renew my passport and fund the trip on my own.

Departing from SFO on American Airlines, I knew that the airline wouldn't have the best wine selection in the world, but when you're traveling in the premium economy section, the vino is free flowing. The in-flight sommelier suggested we pair a lovely cab with our tasty bag of pretzels entree. A few more tiny bottles of this demure wine allowed us to drift off to sleep organically on our transatlantic flight. Next stop: Barcelona.

Sunday, our first official day in Hannah's new country, was a rental car road trip to Cadaques, a delightful seaside town about two hours outside of town. We arrived around noon and immediately sampled a few tapas dishes (tapas is Spanish for a small savory dish). Given that it was a beautiful sunny day sitting on the beachfront patio of a popular restaurant, we shared a pitcher of sangria while staring at the Mediterranean Sea. I'm not a big sangria fan, but hey—when in Rome. (Although by Rome I mean Barcelona.) That night, back in Barcelona, we had our first paella meal of the trip, along with a half bottle of both red and white wine, at a nice family eatery that was but a mere Metro ride away from our hotel.

Monday was all about the hop on/hop off bus tour of the city. We saw every part of Barcelona including Park Güell and C.C Arenas Barcelona, where the professional soccer team FC Barcelona plays. We saw the Olympic Village, the Palau Nacional, the Torry Agbar, Placa Toros Monumental – where they once held actual bull fights before they outlawed bull fighting and turned it into a shopping mall. Shopping can be a lot like a bull fight if there's a good sale going. The tour ended as we passed the Christopher Columbus monument near the Waterfront – which included the historic Old Port. We got off the bus at the Plaza Catalunya, which is the prime shopping district. It's a combination of Union Square (SF) meets Michigan Avenue (Chicago) with a little 5th Avenue (NYC) mixed into Downtown Disney.

That night, after striking out at the first two restaurants we visited, we settled on a Spanish/Greek place and were very pleased with the selection....of wines. Leaning toward a bold red, we ordered the Marques de Cacares and five straws. I'm only kidding, we only had four straws.

Tuesday, we visited the prime landmark in Barcelona, the fabulous Basilica of the Sagrada Familia designed by Antoni Gaudi. This rather large Catholic basilica, because Barcelona already had a cathedral, began construction in 1882 and is expected to be completed by 2026. Like most construction projects, they are slightly behind schedule. After taking a couple photos— a couple hundred, to be precise—we grabbed some lunch before venturing over to our daughter's apartment in the El Camp de L'Alpa del Clot district. Clot is a quieter part of the city, but it's a short walk to the Universidad Autonoma de Barcelona where my little girl is attending classes. Imagine if Hogwarts were a commuter school and you'll get a fitting visual. Luckily I was able to find a school t-shirt in a nearby store, which is a must-have for any collegiate visit.

Being a beautiful evening, we took a friend's suggestion and dined outside at a wonderful restaurant that served, of all things, wine. We stuck with an assortment of tapas dishes and a bottle of Bodegas Vega Sicilia Unico Tinto 2007. I'm only kidding, That wine is $350 a bottle. We stuck with a few pitchers of inexpensive sangria.

Wednesday was a beach day as we walked the Passeig Maritim de la Barceloneta. Talk about a collection of luxury yachts in the harbor. My yacht would seem compact by comparison. From there, we made our way over to the Gothic district (my favorite part of the city). We started at the Cathedral de Barcelona and then strolled the Passeig de Lluis Companys making our way to the Arc de Triomf. My travel party did their share of shopping in and around the Del Mercat de Santa Caterina, which is an intriguing mosaic tiled wavy rooftop marketplace that does not sell meerkats. Too bad, those little critters crack me up. "Mercat" translates as "market."

For dinner, we chose a cool split-level restaurant somewhere near our hotel. We entertained one of Hannah's friends from school by sharing a crisp bottle of white - Martin Codax Arbarino and a spicy bottle of red – Oro Bailen Reserva. Dinner was muchas tapas and paella and dessert was gelato. I was very full walking back to the hotel. Thankfully I brought along my after-dinner lounging pants with an elastic waistband.

Thursday started with a short Metro ride and about an hour train ride to get us to Parc Natural de la Muntana and the Santa Maria de Montserra Abby and Basilica de Montserrat. This is a monastery and basilica built high, high, high up in the mountain with a hairy gondola ride to get to our destination. Luckily the monks served a Marques de Caceres Rioja to calm the nerves of all gondola riders. The grounds are truly amazing, especially given what it must have took to build a town in the side of a rock mountain. Sadly, I'm guessing many donkeys lost their lives hauling building materials 4,055 feet above the valley floor. Apparently, donkeys don't like to ride in gondolas.

That night, for a change of pace, we ate at a lively Mexican restaurant that was filled with college students from all over the United States. I can't say for sure that their margaritas were made of Spanish wine, but after the 5th or 6th it really didn't matter. The meal was delicious, and it was enjoyable watching all the kids having so much fun. That place will be crazy on Cinco de Mayo.

Friday started with a visit to the public market called Mercat St. Josep La Boqueria. We followed our un-Safeway like grocery shopping expedition with a cooking class led by the renowned chef, Carlos Aviles. The culinary excursion was enchanting; however, the paella de marisco (sea food paella) was a little too fishy for my In-N-Out burger-munching pallet. As instructed, because we were in a classroom setting, we washed down our *comida* (food) creations with a few glasses of Gran Feudo, a tangy white wine. We finished the day with a ramble down Las Ramblas, the popular retail promenade. Needless to say, after a decadent afternoon of eating and drinking our self-created Michelin star meal, we opted for a simple dinner of flat bread pizza and a splash of Campo Viejo Tempranillo.

It was wonderful seeing our daughter in her third home, and Barcelona is a truly amazing city worthy of a visit. While we were expecting rain during our visit, because, well you know… . the rain in Spain falls mainly on the plain, we were treated with beautiful weather throughout our weeklong visit. I'm wrapping this piece up as I peruse the isles of BevMo looking for a couple of Spanish wines to add to our tapas-sized wine collection. While I won't be craving paella for a while, I will enjoy a sassy glass of La Riojo Alta Grand Reserva as I download my photos from a wonderful trip to Barca. That's how the locals refer to the town and Hannah is a local now.

22 Time Travel Summer Vacation

While trying to come up with a new summer vacation destination, somewhere other than Tahoe, San Diego or Wally World, I wished I had a time machine. Think of those amazing possibilities. Time travel has always been a popular concept. It was originally popularized by H. G. Wells' 1895 novel *The Time Machine*, which moved the concept of time travel into the public imagination. Imagine, if you will, that you had the ability to travel backward or forward in time to a specific date or period. Think how incredible it would be to teleported from the summer of 2018 to a day/month/year in the past or future, to relive a magical moment, to play a part in history, or to see if flying cars actually materialized, ie; the Hanna-Barbara animated sitcom, *The Jetsons*. What if you could make time travel a summer vacation destination? Pretty cool, right? I wish I could take credit for it, but it was an article idea shared with me by a friend. I wish I could travel back in time and come up with that idea on my own, but I don't think I would use a trip in my super cool time machine just to lay claim to an *ALIVE* article. What a waste. No, when I time travel it's going to be an epic ride with a real purpose in mind.

The major television networks love their weekly series about time travel, and why not? The concept of time travel lends itself to so many great storylines. One of the more popular time travel TV programming shows over the last 20 years is *Timeless*, a series about an unlikely trio who travel through time in order to battle unknown criminals in order to protect history as we know it. *Timeless* is currently running on NBC on Monday nights at 10:00 pm PST. Another hugely popular show was *Quantum Leap* (which ran on NBC from 1989 – 1993) chronicling Dr. Sam Beckett's adventures temporarily taking the place of people to correct historical mistakes showed how time travel could alter or disrupt historical events. However, there are a lot more shows that most viewers might have missed including *Travelers, Making History, Time Trax, Outlander, Flash Forward, Journeyman* and *The Time Tunnel,* to name just a few. I'm not sure if all these series were on NBC, but the brain trust at the Peacock Network seems to have found a popular concept that clicks with the American public.

There have also been countless books written about time travel. By countless, I mean too many to count, literally millions, given my Wiki-research. *A Wrinkle in Time, The Time Travelers Wife, Voyager, Time Bound, Outlander* (again) and *Time and Again* are just a few. One book that I actually read was *11/22/63* by Stephen King, about a time traveler who attempts to prevent the assassination of President John F. Kennedy. This incredibly crafted novel spent sixteen weeks on the New York Times Bestseller list. That King guy has real potential as a writer of novels.

As delightful as these forms of entertainment are, and don't even get me started on the *Back to the Future, Terminator* or *Bill & Ted's Excellent Adventure* movie franchises, I question whether or not the average person, man or woman, given the ability to time travel, would choose to alter history or simply attend a Beatles concert, replay a high school football game, or simply spend time with a deceased loved one? Sure it sounds good to take a week off from work, secure a house/pet sitter and put a hold on the mail, assuming you found a secret portal, flux capacitor or magical hot tub (*Hot Tub Time Machine* was a classic) that could provide you with access to the past or future, would you want to visit Wyatt Earp and Doc Holiday at the OK Corral, visit with your late grandparents as an adolescent or drive a flying car (like George Jetson and Jane, his wife)? There are pros and cons with each, but that's why I write these thought provoking pieces, to challenge you - the reader, to ride with me through this quandary. The following are actual man on the street responses to the following question, If you could access a time machine and spend a week in the past or future, when and where would you go? To be totally honest, they weren't actual random people I found on the street, or homeless street people, but you get my drift.

I wouldn't mind traveling back to the 1950's to see what life was like in a fun and simpler "Happy Days/American Graffiti" time period. No particular time or place, just some random sock hop during that era. Julie C.

I would want to either go back to the late 1960s and spend time in rural Ohio where I grew up or spend a week with my children as toddlers again. Erin D.

I would like to visit Sicily, Italy in the mid-1800s to see what my grandparents (both sides) were like as children. Mary Jo DM.

I would travel back to the stock market crash of Black Monday on October 19, 1987. I would spend the entire week loading the boat with smart stock buys that would set me up for life. Eric O.

I would go back to my senior year of high school and tell teenage me not to date the guy I ended up seeing for three years. I was at a crossroads and made the wrong choice back then and that decision altered my life. Nicole O.

I might travel forward to see if some of the Black Mirror episodes actually came true. Vanisha K.

I would spend a week with Jesus in Jerusalem or Galileo. Sean C.

I would blast 20-30 years in the future to make sure my kids are doing Ok. Either that or attend Woodstock in 1969. Jim L.

I would travel back to 5th grade (1970) to the skating rink in Melbourne, Florida where I asked the cutest girl in our class, Robin Thompson, to slow skate and then lost the nerve to hold her hand. I've always regretted that missed opportunity. Blake C.

I'm an Olympics junkie and would travel back to the 1980 Winter Olympics in Lake Placid, New York. It would be the week that the "Miracle on Ice" U.S. men's hockey team beat the

Soviet Union in the semi-finals and then beat Finland to win the gold. Eva G.

Before our children were born, my husband and I visited Paris for the first time. Paris was somewhere I had always wanted to visit, I had studied French in school and we were madly in love. That's what I would like to do again because it was such a magical time. Vanessa C.

So I guess it's my turn. As tempting as it would be to be at one of my more memorable high school or college football games, I would use my chance to travel back to 1988 when both of my parents were still alive. I would take with me tons of pictures of their granddaughters, Hannah and Claire, who they never got a chance to meet. I would spend time asking them all the questions I wish I had asked, but never did. I would also pay strict attention to all their stories I only half listened to or rolled my eyes through the first time I semi-heard them. I would watch their favorite shows or listen to their radio stations with them without bitching and complaining like I used to do. I would gorge on my mom's great home cooking (think Paula Dean) and ask my dad to walk me through some basic home improvement skills (think MacGyver). Without getting too sentimental, we all missed so much by not having them around all these years and I would give anything, even the top-secret plans to my super cool time machine, for a chance to spend just one week with them again.

For any of my contemporaries in the fifty-to-sixty-year-old demographic, I encourage you to read the book *Stingray Afternoons* by Steve Rushin. Rushin's memoir vividly describes life and times in the 1970s growing up in the greater Minneapolis area. His magical depiction of pop culture during that era will take you back to your suburban youth. I have recommended this book to the guys I went to elementary school with, including Mark Peterson, Ron Mendez, Ron Hood, Derek Sousa, Jeff

Morales and Luis Pena as well as the neighborhood kids I grew up with such as Chris Fowlie, Terry Ivie, Carlo and Victor Martina, Renny Del Carlo and Albie Cavagnaro. As Rushin points out, your school friends and your neighborhood friends rarely crossed over so it was completely acceptable to have two sets of best buddies. Those who have read it love to call and recant similar our own "Stingray" experiences growing up in the shadow of Moffett Field Naval Air Base in beautiful Mountain View (long before it became Google View). In the absence of actual time travel, this book was the next best thing. I hope you find your own personal method of time travel this summer, when and wherever you choose to go.

23 Whatever Happened to Customer Service? The Sequel

Back in March of 2008, I wrote an article for *ALIVE* entitled "Whatever Happened to Customer Service?" After years of dealing with rude, arrogant, selfish, distracted and hopelessly ambivalent frontline employees, I decided to voice my displeasure to corporate America. Like many of my friends, I was so tired of feeling unimportant, unappreciated and invisible to those who were taking my money that I spoke out for the masses. The masses may be a bit of an overstatement—maybe just a few friends, my sister and a second cousin on my dad's side.

As a self-proclaimed connoisseur of customer service, I am constantly rating my CS experiences at restaurants, financial institutions and retail stores. My wife and kids will tell you that I've been known to rate the customer service I get from our spa service technician, my dentist and the people who work at the Oakland-Alameda Coliseum/Arena. Just for the record, I love my dentist! A big shout-out to Melanie Koehler, DDS and her staff in Danville. They are outstanding. I'm also known to regularly assess the service I get from the various airlines, rent-a-car agencies and hotels when I travel. I'm one of those old school guys (because I'm old) who believes if I'm spending my hard-earned money to pay for a good, service or experience, then I should be treated well by the employees working for my business, unless I'm being a tool - which I try not to be for whatever that's worth. However, that brings up a good point. Let's face it, the customer is not <u>always</u> right. There are more than a fair share of malcontents, scammers and grifters out there trying to get over on unsuspecting businesses. Additionally, we live in a very litigious society. Therefore, while there should always be a high priority placed on customer service, I'll understand if there's a "once burned twice shy" underlying edict at work. I would just hate to see anything undermine a company's CS based corporate culture.

While I was beginning to feel that customer service was becoming a lost art when my original article came out nine years ago, I'm here to tell you that I'm encouraged by the resurgence in customer care and the fine art of servicing your customers with respect and appreciation. Somewhere (*ALIVE* Magazine - March 2008), the word got out that the buying public was sick of being ignored, shunned and minimalized and the time was right to turn that ship around. In this Millennial "Me Generation" it's good to see the more sophisticated executive management teams from a good number of companies are prioritizing customer service again.

Customer service is something that I feel should be addressed at every level of an organization. If I ran a company such as Copeland Tech, Copeland's Pet Emporium or McCopeland's Irish Pub, once I hired a new employee I would enroll him or her in our Customer Service University (Go CSU). Before they could interact with my customers, they would have to complete their degree. Promotions would require an advanced degree. On day one, phrases such as "Hello, we'll be with you in just a minute," "Thank you for waiting, we appreciate your business," and "Please come again" would be built into the culture. We would likely also add, "If you like us on FB or post a positive review on Yelp and you'll receive a discount coupon for your next visit". I would periodically send in shills to rate their customer experience so that I could weed out the flunkies. Every organization has its share of flunkies or non-conformers and they need to be purged. Not from the planet, just from a frontline position of working with customers.

"Ownership encourages us to think of our customers as guests. Our goal is to ensure our guests are treated like family. At the start of every season, part of our staff development is to instill trust in each other and trust from our guests." —Johanna Wilson, Guest Relations Director, Bridge Bay at Shasta Lake

In my original article, being so much younger and impetuous, I had no reservations about throwing a company under the bus if their employees displayed poor or non-existent customer service habits. That included Circuit City, AT&T, Abercrombie & Fitch and American Express. While some of those companies are still in business, others that disappointed me, such as Sports Authority, Washington Mutual Bank, Macaroni Grill and Radio Shack seem to have had trouble surviving. Is there any direct correlation? I don't think so. Don't even get me started on the DMV or US Postal Service.

In that article, I also complimented numerous large companies that had placed an emphasis on training their employees to treat the customer with respect and gratitude. That included Safeway, Sugar Bowl Ski Resort, San Francisco Giants/AT&T Park and Wells Fargo Bank. This was obviously before Wells opened millions of fake accounts for their unsuspecting customers. That's no bueno in the customer service world.

Needless to say, an emphasis on serving the customer starts at the top. Every successful CEO knows the importance of maintaining customer loyalty through exemplary customer service. Titans of industry such as Richard Branson, Elon Musk and Tim Cook may not have returned any of my calls for this article, but that doesn't mean they don't recognize that need for their frontline employees to be nice to me and make me feel appreciated and smart and special. Virgin, Tesla and Apple all do a wonderful job of training their personnel and my experiences have been great with these companies, although to date all I've done at

Tesla is waste their sales peoples' time, but (fingers crossed) one of these days I will be an actual buyer.

Recognition goes out to the following local companies/people who make customer service a priority every day. Greg Meier of Diablo Motors and his staff go out of the way to make a prospective car buyer feel important and appreciated. Kurt Chambliss at TMC Financing and Matt Cheeseman at City National Bank should both win awards for how well they interface with clients and how they lead by example with their respective teams. Both Greg Vella at Alpine Awards and Karen Cordeiro of Danville Bakery are to be commended for their willingness to go above and beyond at every turn and their commitment to the community. Finally, Jennifer Burton at Interior Motions (a workplace workspace company) could teach a graduate class in customer service at CS University. She may be the best I've ever seen at showing appreciation and taking care of her clients. Finally, Gotta Eat a Pita, AutoTech and Dublin Jewelers have all shown that they know the meaning of good customer service.

If we go with the basic definition of customer service, that being that it is the art of taking care of the customer's needs by providing and delivering professional, helpful, high quality service and assistance before, during, and after the customer's requirements are met, then I'm happy to report that apparently it's an additional core value that's been added to a lot more company's mission statements and that makes this customer feels like he was heard way back when.

24 Where Does the Time Go?

It's said, time flies when you're having fun, but I'm finding that time flies even when I'm not having fun. Time flies when I'm happy or sad, busy or bored, burdened or carefree, having the time of my life or writing another article for ALIVE. By the time you read this article, it will be Valentine's Day. I haven't even taken down my Christmas tree and now it's time for flowers, cards, chocolates, jewelry, fine wine and/or fancy dinners out. Just for the record, I'm always very appreciative of any of these romantic gifts/gestures from my loyal readers. Don't be shy. It seems like just yesterday, we were celebrating Hanukah, Christmas and New Year's Eve. For me that's especially true as the Chief sets my deadlines unrealistically early for the magazine so here I am on January 2nd trying to come up with a piece for the February issue. That said, time has a way of speeding up when we most need it to slow down. I only got 24 hours yesterday, how many did you get?

In the song *Young Turks*, Rod Stewart sang, "Because life is so brief and time is a thief when you're undecided. And like a fistful of sand, it can slip right through your hands." That Rod is deep.

Growing up, time moved at what seemed like a normal pace. Days were from sun up to sun down, evenings and weekends were leisurely, summer vacation from school was a legit 12 weeks and it seemed like forever until Christmas or my next birthday rolled around. I never thought much about time as a kid and yet time is a constant topic of conversation as an adult.

In the song, *Time Stands Still*, by Rush, Geddy Lee sang, "Time stands still, I'm not looking back, but I want to look around me now. Time stands still, see more of the people and the places that surround me now." Geddy could be very introspective. Probably because he's from Canada.

Once I became an adult, time seemed to speed up. It started a little at a time, but days, weeks and months all started to go by a little quicker. A busy workweek would fly by in the blink of an eye. A weeklong vacation would feel like it was over before it even started. Every six-month dental check up and teeth cleaning seemed to arrive before I got into a regular flossing routine.

In the song *Time is on My Side*, by the Rolling Stones, Mick sang, "Time, time, time is on my side, yes it is, I said time, time, time is on my side, yes it is, I said time, time, time is on my side." We get it Mick. He's always been more than a little conceited.

When I became a young parent, when my children were newborns and then toddlers, each day seemed to last forever, but somehow we started going through calendars at a rapid pace. As someone once said about having children, the days are long and the years fly by, No truer words have ever been spoken. Then, the next thing I knew, my kids were teenagers and I worried about them all the time. They were also so busy I barely had enough time to get anything done outside of keeping them on schedule.

In the song, *Cats in the Cradle*, Harry Chapin sings the ultimate song about the passage of time as it relates to parenting. I would go on, but that song chokes me up every time I hear it and a writer isn't supposed to cry.

When we were attending the kid's sporting events, a swim meet or equestrian horse competition, they seemed to wipe out an entire weekend. I once saw a t-shirt that read, "If I only had one day left to live, I'd want to spend it at a swim meet because that feels like the longest day on earth." Take it from me, a horse show feels even longer.

Now my wife and I are empty nesters. Where did the time go? With our two girls away at college, time has new meaning. There's way too much time between visits, but time goes by pretty quickly just trying to keep up with tuition and other expenses.

In the song *Time in a Bottle,* Jim Croce sang, "There never seems to be enough time, to do the things you want to do. I've looked around enough to know, that you're the one I want to go, through time with". Jim sure knew how to sweet-talk a lady.

In the song, *(I've had) The Time of My Life,* Bill Medley and Jennifer Warnes sang, "Now I've had the time of my life/ No, I never felt like this before/ Yes I swear it's the truth/ And I owe it all to you. Cause I've had the time of my life and I owe it all to you. I still get goose bumps picturing Baby and Johnny tearing up the Catskills banquet room with their provocative dance moves.

At work, a day can fly by or it drag out forever. When we're busy, there's never enough time and when it's slow, there's too much time. Days lead to weeks, weeks to months and then another year is gone. Because a large majority of us *work to live* and not *live to work,* the workday can't end soon enough to enjoy the quality time we all want, need and crave.

In the song, *Long Time,* by Boston, the band sang, "It's been such a long time/I think I should be goin', yeah time doesn't wait for me, it keeps on rollin'. And then, Well, I'm takin' my time, I'm just movin' on, you'll forget about me after I've been gone. And I take what I find, I don't want no more. It's just outside of why our front door." Those 80's bands were full of long haired guys that just lived for the moment.

The one and only exception I can come up with to time moving too rapidly is probably "doing time". You know, jail time. Being locked-up, aka doing time in the big house, the joint, hoose-gow or the gray bar hotel. However you want to phrase it, prison time has got to be the most difficult surreal time experience a person can face. I've seen The Shawshank Redemption, The Green Mile, Escape from Alcatraz and The Longest Yard so I know. Doing time seems like just that, doing it. Not spending time, not killing time, not even wasting time. Time has got to take on a completely different meaning when you're locked in a cell.

In the song, *Does Anyone Really Know What Time It Is*, by the band Chicago, the guys sang, "As I was walking down the street one day, a man came up to me and asked me what the time was that was on my watch and I said…Does anybody really know what time it is? Does anybody really care? If so I can't imagine why/we've all got time enough to cry." Personally, I don't usually cry when I look at my Timex, but the band sure sold a crap ton of records with that line.

As we celebrate Valentine's Day, knowing that Groundhog Day, St. Patrick's Day, Passover/Easter, National Puppy Day, the First Day of Spring, Spring Break, Daylight Savings and Mother's Day are right around the corner, take time to smell the roses. Slow things down enough to enjoy the moment. Stop rushing around long enough to savor the time spent with family and friends or doing something that you love. We only get so much time in our life, so don't waste it.

In the song *Time after Time*, Cyndi Lauper sang, "Time after time, Time after time, Time after time, Time after time, Time after time, Time after time, Time after time, Time after, Time". I don't know about you, but I find Cyndi to be a bit repetitive.

25 What's It Like to be ....

My good friend, Michael Guida, has an interesting idea for a podcast series, asking people what it's like to do what they do for a career or hobby. People—well, loyal fans of my monthly column—routinely ask me (once a year if I'm lucky), what's it like to be a humor lifestyle columnist for a popular and trendy regional magazine. It's actually a lot of fun if you don't mind criticism and ridicule, and that's just from my family and friends. I like to tell people that it's a labor of love, which it is because it's certainly not a labor of riches. I find writing my little article cathartic. It allows me to tap into my creative side which is a contrast to my day job as a commercial real estate agent where, at time creativity is needed, but mostly it's just a grind it out sales and numbers game. If I didn't have these articles, I would be forced to take up scrap booking, hair styling or inappropriate origami to relieve myself of all those creative juices coursing through my veins.

That said, it got me thinking of what some other people do and what it must be like to possess or experience their unique profession, hobby or skill. This got me started along my path and, well, another amazing magazine piece. My subjects were chosen based on my interest level and access to them. I would love to know what's it like to be a two time NBA MVP, but I don't have Steph's email address and the Warriors have repeatedly asked me to stop calling their offices.

So, what's it like to be . . .

The Mayor of Danville – *Renee Morgan (current City Council Member and former Mayor):* The hours are long and the days off are few, but the honor to serve and advocate for the residents of Danville and maintain the character of our community are beyond measure. As an elected official it is important to be dedicated to the vision and integrity of our constituents. We truly live in a special place. After living in Danville for 30 years and raising my children here I plan to keep it this way.

A Rock Star – *David Victor (formerly of Boston):* Being onstage, performing classic hit rock songs for thousands of music lovers, and delivering the goods, is an exhilarating, transcendent feeling. Fans love the music, and it's an honor to make it. It's a real bummer when you have an "off" night, and you know it! There's nothing like being there, for both performer and fan. Videos pale in comparison. Capturing the moment and making the magic is a "presence thing." Traveling by plane or bus from city to city is as romantic as anything I've ever experienced (professionally speaking, of course!) Having a "Performer Pass", and going anywhere you want in the venue without anyone in a yellow windbreaker giving you any grief, is totally rock n roll. It's a tough way to make a living, but nothing I've ever experienced professionally is as rewarding. I'm writing these thoughts down as I'm flying down to LA for a gig.

The Owner of a Comedy Club – *Gayle Thomas of Tommy T's:* It absolutely has to be one of the best jobs in the world to work in an environment where you provide laughter. I've heard it said that laughter is medicine for the soul, so I guess I'm pretty much a doctor. Ok, maybe that's going too far, but if I could write prescriptions for people to take a break from their daily grind to come sit down for two hours and forget their troubles while laughing, I'd hand those out like candy on Halloween.

A Stand-up Comedian – *Bryan Kellen:* It goes from being frightening, frustrating, embarrassing, humiliating, depressing, lonely and hard, to comforting, uncomplicated, shameless, glorifying, thrilling, effortless. . . every damn night you're on stage.

A Song Writer – *Paul Jefferson* (Co-wrote "That's as Close as I'll get to Loving You," a #1 hit for Aaron Tippin and "You're Not My God" with Keith Urban). It's like playing the lottery where you must buy your ticket from the top of Mount Everest. . . but when you hear one of your songs on the car radio the first time you realize it was worth losing a few fingers.

A Commercial Airline Pilot – *Captain John Macholz of American Airlines*: Despite being completely sober, I never know what day of the week it is or what city I'm in. I also can't make plans this month to attend an event next month. But seriously, I'm about to upgrade to the Boeing 787 Dreamliner – a 335-passenger international wide body twin engine jet airliner. This is my childhood dream came true. I love the view from my office and the ability to travel with my family. I am incredibly blessed.

A Policeman/First Responder – *Dave Peruzzaro, Captain with the San Mateo Police Deptt:* Being a law enforcement first responder truly is a job like no other. You never know what the next call for service has in store for you. One moment you are on routine patrol and the next moment you could find yourself in a life changing event. You can't un-see the tragedy you see or change the experiences you experience. While the job of a police officer and first responder is an emotional roller coaster, it's an honorable, challenging and incredibly rewarding profession.

A Livermore Valley Winery Tasting Room Pourer– *Michele Milz of Darcy Kent*: Unpredictable, but always fun, and yet sometimes even a bit stressful. Meeting people is where the fun comes in! Some of them are the most experienced wine drinkers;

for others it may be their twenty-first birthday, looking for their first sip of alcohol (wink wink). Then of course, there's everyone else in between: Bachelorette parties, 50th birthday celebrations, class reunions, and the out-of-towners visiting California wine country for the first time. The people you meet make the job easy and fun because the act of wine tasting is, in fact, fun! My favorite types of customers are the ones who ask questions and test my own knowledge of wine. Sometimes I even learn a thing or two about wine in the hour I spend with a customer.

A Professional Auctioneer – *Damon Casatico of Charity Benefit Auctions***:** Being the center of attention and running a big and/or high-profile charity auction with dozens of high priced fundraising items is like conducting a symphony or being an air traffic controller with your hair on fire!

A Football Coach - *Aaron Becker of San Ramon Valley High School:* Being the Varsity Head Football Coach at SRVHS is a tremendous honor, not to mention a year round job. Our program prides itself on developing young men of great character and whether it be during football season, winter weight lifting, or spring and summer training we are constantly working toward that end, not to mention winning football games! As a former "Wolf" myself (class of '97) its very rewarding to see our young men move on to bigger and better things beyond high school and it's still exhilarating to run on to the field every Friday night for a big game. Like any job being the head football coach at SRVHS has its ups and downs, but the relationships formed and the memories created each and every season make it all worthwhile!

A Photographer – *Krista Keller* (specializing in High School Senior Photos)**:** It's hard work, but it feels great because I get the chance to make kids feel special and confident for a day. This most likely is the last time they will have professional photos taken until they get married.

A Master Skydiver - *Steve Caltagirone (over 1000 jumps):* "For me, skydiving provides the perfect combination of two experiences that would otherwise stand in opposition of one another. On the one hand, jumping out of a plane offers true sensory overload mixed with a steroid-dose of good old-fashioned adrenaline! On the other hand, it offers a level of peace many skydivers struggle to describe in words. The pure endorphin rush of plummeting to the earth at speeds exceeding 120 m.p.h. speaks for itself. Within this adrenaline-fueled excitement, however, lies a layer of inner peace and tranquility that is almost spiritual in nature. In the immortal words of one Leonardo da Vinci: "Once you have tasted flight, you will forever walk the earth with your eyes turned skyward. For there you have been, and there you will long to return."

A Magazine and Book Publisher - *Eric Johnson, Alive Media and Books*: Being a publisher of books and a monthly magazine is like being the Wizard of Oz. I get to use what appear to many to be "magical" powers, taking authors' and writers' work and transforming it, then putting it into different formats—printed and digital books and magazines—that reach thousands of readers throughout the Bay Area (in the case of ALIVE Magazine) and the entire world (in the case of ALIVE Books). *And...* and I get to do it all whilst hiding behind a curtain so that no one really knows how we do it or who I am!

It goes without saying that I have some incredibly interesting and talented friends. A logical question is what are they doing hanging out with me? This was an incredibly fun assignment and I look forward to a follow up piece. Take my work for it when I say, you won't be disappointed if you take the time to ask your friends or family members, what's it like to be. . .

Great idea, Michael Guida.

26 You're not a Millennial if .....

Wikipedia, not me, defines **millennials** (also known as Generation Y, Generation Me, Echo Boomers and Peter Pan Generation) as the demographic cohort following Generation X. There are no precise dates for when this cohort (they used that word twice) starts or ends; demographers and researchers typically use the early 1980s as starting birth years and ending birth years ranging from the late-1990s. This puts the average millennial in the age range of 20 – 36 years old. The term was apparently coined in 1987 by authors William Strauss and Neil Howe, likely as a way to identify a subculture of soon-to-be tech savvy, coffee consuming, battery-powered-car driving, designer label wearing, EDM festival raging, hair product jellying, no body fat trending, self-absorbed narcissists. Don't get me wrong, I have a lot of friends and business associates who identify as a millennial. For gosh sakes, my niece and nephews are the m-word, but if you want to know the truth, as a whole, millennials can be really annoying.

Personally, I'm a hybrid of two intersecting generations, the tail end of the Baby Boomers and the beginning of Generation X. "Boomers," described again by the people at Wikipedia, are the demographic group born during the post–World War II baby boom, approximately between the years 1946 and 1962. As a group, Baby Boomers were the wealthiest, most active, and most physically fit generation up to the era in which they arrived and were amongst the first to grow up genuinely expecting the world to improve with time. Whereby Gen X are Wiki-defined as children who were raised during a time of shifting societal values and as children were sometimes called the "latchkey generation," due to reduced adult supervision compared to previous generations. They also dealt with increasing divorce rates and increased maternal participation in the workforce prior to widespread availability of childcare options outside of the home. Research describes Gen X adults (1963 – 1982) as active, happy, and as achieving a work-life balance. The cohort has been credited with entrepreneurial tendencies. I'm not saying that both the Boomers and Gen Xers don't have their share of losers, but as a whole, our Gen-blend has accomplished some cool stuff. Perhaps you've heard of Jon Stewart, Garth Brooks, Paula Abdul, Jerry Rice, Kate Spade, Steve Carell, Bo Jackson, Tom Cruise, John Bon Jovi, MC Hammer, Jodie Foster, Bobcat Goldthwait and Chris Christie. Like me, all were born in 1962. Getting back to the millennial generation, I've made a few observations about this demographic and come to the conclusion that:

You're Not a Millennial if . . .
—You work in an industry other than tech, international finance, sports entertainment, craft brewing or "growing"
—You aren't on a first name basis with your barista
—Your coffee order has less than three words
—You've ever made a pot of coffee
—Your preferred mode of transportation doesn't involve a Clipper Card
—You wear glasses because they help you see
—You don't consider playing X Box participating a sport
—You go home from the club before last call
—You've ever washed your own car
—You've actually popped the hood of a car
—You mow your own lawn
—You have a lawn
—You've ever written a letter
—Your definition of being a gamer is a reference to softball or bowling
—Your favorite vacation destination involves an RV

— Hydrating your body means something other than upping your shots count on a Friday night
— Your music collection consists of anything besides obscure European EDM DJs
— Your hope of a new car is something other than an Uber XL Max.
— You prefer to be at home as opposed to the office
— You don't consider your smart phone a physical appendage of your body
— You use your smart phone mostly for phone calls
— You spend more than the three major holidays (Thanksgiving, Christmas/Hanukah and Easter/Passover) and a few birthdays with your immediate family
— You can easily go to bed without one last look at your inbox
— You don't suffer withdrawals if you haven't downloaded anything in more than a day
— You haven't taken a selfie at a wedding, funeral or during a medical procedure

My father was part of The Greatest Generation (*The Greatest Generation* is the title of a 1998 book by American journalist Tom Brokaw, which popularized the term "Greatest Generation" to describe those who grew up in the United States during the deprivation of the Great Depression, and then went on to fight in World War II). USN Chief Petty Officer Steven Copeland would roll over in his grave if he saw how millennials seem to lack common everyday life skills because most are so driven to create the next (totally unnecessary) mobile app designed for gamers that will appeal to a VC with aspirations of taking it public, that they're too busy to learn how to change a tire.

Don't get me wrong, I appreciate the millennial generation for the advancements they will likely bring to our future. It will probably be a millennial who invents the affordable flying car, recreational time travel and a cure for cancer. It might also be a millennial who organizes a *Friends* reunion show featuring the entire cast. If David Schwimmer doesn't attend, it's not a full cast!

Each generation in our country has offered something different to our cultural landscape, our American fabric or the structure of our lives. How we define their contributions is immaterial. If the millennial generation ends up kicking ass on The Greatest Generation, Baby Boomers and Gen X then good for them because as a country we win. That said, I wish they would try to be a little less annoying in the process.

II
Dad Speak
Observations and Advice from Dad

I don't proclaim to know everything when it comes to parenting, but I do know that I have an endless supply of love, the desire to always improve and a never-say-quit attitude. For these reasons, I feel the freedom to sprinkle dad dust on my readers. My articles related to parenting and more specifically being a father, a dad, a padre, a papa or a pappy are firsthand accounts of issues I have experienced. To the best of my recollection my children have never called me or referred to me as pappy, but they could if they felt the urge.

Being a dad involves so many things. Not just being there for your kids to provide love, sustenance and protection, but to set an example, provide advice and take care of the pets they said they would take care of even though you knew they never would, but you said yes anyway knowing full well that you would feed and walk the animals, scoop the poop, change the litter box, clean the cages and bury the deceased.

My little girls are growing up too fast

My oldest daughter just turned eighteen years old. That's approximately 6,570 days since she showed up. Where did the time go? It seems like just yesterday that we were bringing her home from the hospital in a car seat that was more than likely not secured properly. Someone once said, "The days are long and the years fly by." Truer words have never been spoken. It seems surreal to fully comprehend that my baby is old enough to, among other things, serve in the military, rent a car, initiate legal action, buy a lottery ticket and purchase a house. Additionally, in November of 2016, she'll be able to vote for Donald Trump, Hillary Clinton or whomever she feels will best serve the office as President of the United States. It seems like just yesterday she was deciding on which of her American Girl dolls would get to go on vacation with us.

The year was 1997, and on a crisp fall day in October, after eighteen hours of labor, my wife and I were blessed with a beautiful baby girl. I'll freely admit that my wife did most of the heavy lifting that day, but I did secure more than my share of ice chips. Hannah (a name we both loved) Kathryn (after my mother) Copeland came into the world at approximately 10:42 pm. As excited as we both were to meet her, I did appreciate that we were able to watch most of the Giants/Dodgers game while we waited for her arrival. Once she showed up we laughed, we cried and I thanked God that she was healthy and safe.

Once we brought Hannah Banana home from the hospital, without an instruction manual no less, we were quick to realize that we knew virtually nothing about raising an infant. We spent a fair amount of time those first few days on the phone with the advice nurse from Valley-Care Medical Center. Luckily, we had met several wonderful families in our Lamaze class who also didn't know anything about infants so together we muddled through those first few months. There's strength in numbers. Despite our bumbling and fumbling, our little miracle ate, slept and pooped her way to becoming a toddler, then a little girl, a tween and ultimately a teenager. Today, as a young adult, she continues to amaze me every day.

In 1999, we were blessed once again with a second daughter. Claire (another name we both loved) Diane (a favorite aunt of my wife) Copeland was born on a warm summer day in July at approximately 10:42 am. When we arrived at the hospital around 8:00 am the day of her arrival, we naturally assumed we had a full day of contractions (breathing, screaming and ice chips) before we would make her acquaintance. Little did we know, she had other plans and before I could even unpack our soothing Kenny G CD, she was lying under the incubator lights due to a touch of jaundice. I dare not mention her crossed eyes. Fortunately for Claire Bear, this wasn't our first rodeo. Her sister had taught us so much about nursing, changing, bathing and the soothing tranquility of a bouncy chair, that we were almost professionals the second time around. Her maturation has also progressed with astonishing speed. She too has become a teenager and just this past summer took up the sport of driving. Am I the only one that thinks sixteen years old is too young to operate a moving vehicle independently? Can't we all agree that a full year of tandem driving with a learner's permit would be a good thing? What's the rush?

At the risk of oversimplifying, being a parent is a tremendous amount of work. It's a never-ending stream of long days, sleep deprived nights, chauffeur-filled weeks, entertaining and exhausting vacations, difficult phases and plenty of growing pains. Fortunately, there's also more joy than you could ever think humanly possible. In my evolution from Diaper Genie to curling irons, bath time to privacy in the bathroom, bedtime to curfews, play dates to real dates, first words to smart-phones, alphabet to SAT, strollers to tricycles, scooters to bikes and first steps to driver license, the time has flown by in the blink of an eye. When I look back on photos covering the past eighteen years, I remember my parents saying appreciate every day and somehow I didn't. At times, I long for the innocence, the unconditional love and tender moments that I shared when my girls were little. Innocence lost is a term that I have come to appreciate as they begin to face real-life struggles and challenges that come with age.

Don't get me wrong, I am enjoying where my girls are at this stage of their lives. Hannah is enjoying the various activities connected to her senior year of high school, considering her college options and working a job. Claire is a junior, a dynamite swimmer and an equally good student. Both girls have a witty sense of humor, are respectful and responsible and act maturely except when they don't. We can talk about a wide variety of world topics (politics, sports, religion), but we had a few equally interesting conversations when the topics were Barbies, Play-Doh and all things Disney. Did you know that Play-Doh was first introduced to public schools in Cincinnati, Ohio, as a modeling compound, in the mid-1950s?

The supersonic progression of the girl's school years is what amazes me the most. As quickly as elementary school (K-5) flew by, the three years of middle school are a blur. Fortunately, thanks to Friday night football and basketball games, proms and homecomings, driver's education and college applications, the time from freshman to senior year is somewhat more interactive for parents.

To my friends with sons who have a different set of rules, obstacles and concerns, time does not move slower for them. It has been said that raising girls is easier when they are young and more difficult as they get older and boys are the opposite. Regardless of whether this is true, children are children and they all grow up too fast. A lyric from the song "Young Turks," by the legendary Rod Stewart, goes something like, "Life is so brief and time is a thief, when you're undecided and like a fist full of sand it can slip right through your hand." I have no doubt that this is how Billy Ray Cyrus feels every time he watches his daughter Miley in *Hannah Montana* reruns.

One day in the not-too-distant future, I will assuredly long for the memories of this time in my daughters' lives. When they are eventually married with children of their own, I'll undoubtedly miss these teenage years. It probably goes without saying that we should all appreciate that our children are growing up and there's nothing we can do to slow down the march of time. I may just be a simple Twitter philosopher, but I believe we should live, laugh and love with our kids and appreciate every minute together. Whatever time in their lives that should happen to be.

I'm Not as Frugal as My Father

My dad was frugal. Frugal is a nice word for cheap. Steven D. Copeland was an emotionally generous guy, but the generosity ceased when it came to spending money. Halloween was a good example of his frugalness. Every October 31st, he and my mom would turn out the lights in our house, pretending not to be at home, while they sent us kids out into the neighborhood to replenish their candy supply. He carved a jack-o-lantern out of an orange from the neighbor's tree.

Halloween is a wonderful holiday and costumes are a big part of the festivities. People, old and young alike, spending ungodly amounts of money on the most elaborate costumes imaginable just to make a statement or grab some attention.

That was unacceptable to my dad. To my dad, Halloween costumes were a needless waste of money. He would say, "Mike (that's what he called me), anyone with half a brain and some imagination should be able to come up with a costume using crap from around the house." My dad was very profound. There was no way Mr. Copeland was going to take out a loan at the Halloween Super Store just to dazzle his co-workers with an authentic Batman costume at the annual company Exotic Erotic Ball. For five years in a row, I was a variation of brown paper bagman. I was paper bag hobo, paper bag knight, paper bag robot, paper bag cowboy and paper bag pimp. I was a plaid sheeted ghost a few times too. When I was in college, I'll admit to resurrecting paper bag pimp. I was straight up paper bag pimping when I convinced a few sorority girls to dress as paper bag hookers. It was a hoot.

Looking back, I assume my dad was so frugal because he grew up during the Great Depression. For those of you clueless millennial kids, the Great Depression took place between 1929 and the late 1930s. It was a cosmic combination of Black Monday (the stock market crash of 1987) intersecting with the mortgage fallout of 2008 (Think *The Big Short* meets *Too Big To Fail*), but much worse. Somehow my dad always seemed like he was preparing for the Great Depression Part II. I truly didn't know the depths of my father's frugalness until I became an adult. Before that, I just assumed what he told me was the actual truth when it came to monitoring our household expenses. The following is an example of what we experienced as youths.

My dad frequently asked for price checks at the Dollar Store.

My dad would never pay for a Mt. Diablo campsite permit, so during the summers we crashed overnight at Osage Park. He told me the baseball dugouts were chain link caves. Fortunately for us, the goose hunting was plentiful.

My dad was passionate about finding a good deal, which explains his Christmas shopping excursions to every garage sale in town.

When we were little kids, instead of taking us to the Monterey Bay Aquarium, he took us to the Dreager's fish and fresh meat department. While I thought it was natural for the majestic swordfish to sleep on a bed of ice, I did wonder why the halibut was breaded.

Instead of taking us to the Oakland Zoo, we would visit the local SPCA. I was seven before I learned that our Terrier wasn't an aardvark.

My dad used to brag that we had waterfront property, but that was only when our septic tank would back up.

The only time we went swimming during the summer was when we took a dip in the lake at Oak Hill Park.

Going to the drive-in meant sitting in our lawn chairs while watching the neighbors' TV through their plate glass window and eating un-popped popcorn from their bird feeder.

My dad wanted me to learn an instrument and convinced me, after years of practice, that the kazoo was an integral part of every orchestra.

Our "vacation" was a new disk for our Viewfinder.

When we went to the park the ducks would throw bread at us.

Kids from Third World countries sent us money.

Our black and white TV had two channels, On and Off and I was his remote control.

My baseball cleats were actually tennis shoes with nails hammered through the soles.

Going out to dinner always included the phrase, "do you want fries with that?"

Instead of getting a chemistry set for my birthday, my dad just gave me a set of test tube shot glasses from Chili's and a Bunsen burner in the shape of a Bic lighter.

When I asked for Nike tennis shoes, what I got was a pair of Keds with the "swoosh" drawn on with a Sharpie.

At my mother's annual company holiday party, we were the Adopt-a-Family.

My dad routinely "borrowed" office supplies from his work and he was self-employed.

If my dad had been at the Last Supper, he would have asked for separate checks.

I once asked my dad to borrow fifty bucks. His response was, "Forty dollars? I haven't got thirty. What do you need twenty for?"

It goes without saying that as an adult I appreciate my father's life lessons about the value of a dollar. I may be a little freer spending than the old man, but it's not like I have tech stock IPO earnings to throw around on crazy purchases. If I desire a good or service, I instinctively price shop, looking for a bargain. I'm not afraid to negotiate for the most favorable terms. It's not even beneath me to pretend I don't speak or understand English.

This Halloween, I'm thinking of rocking a new paper bag costume, sassy magazine columnist. I'll be party-hopping. Instead of paying ten cents for paper bags at Safeway, I plan to use my recycled grocery bags to reduce my carbon footprint and save the planet. I'll be the guy wearing the Trader Joes/Bev Mo/Goodwill canvas bags. Make sure you have plenty of Twix and Milky Way on hand at your party as I plan to stock up. I'll also take a carton of milk, a loaf of bread and a dozen eggs if you really want to treat me right. As I learned from my dad, they won't say

3 The Prospective College Road Show

Oh, to be a high school junior living along the I-680 corridor. A typical East Bay high school junior who is between sixteen and seventeen years old has a mobile smart phone, a computer and probably just came into possession of a nice car. He, she or they are undoubtedly seriously thinking about their college options. Life is good and they have the world in front of them. I acknowledge that their class load, friends, work, extra-curricular activities and issues with parents (forgive us for loving you so much) can be a bit challenging, but if they play their cards right, in two short years they'll be heading off to the college of their choice. College selection ranks as one of the most important decisions a young person is asked to make. A college degree positively impacts a person's self-esteem, employability and earning potential. Not to mention, it serves to eventually sever the financial umbilical cord from their parents.

My family and I are planning a visit to the University of Arizona and Arizona State. **Kacy H., MVHS Class of 2016**

A great many families will be incorporating college campus tours into their upcoming vacations. Our family, who will be heading to Texas for Thanksgiving, has already scheduled school visits at Southern Methodist University, Texas Christian University and Baylor University. Call us odd (everyone else does), but ever since we visited Harvard University while in Boston about ten years ago, our family has tried to incorporate a campus tour whenever and wherever we've been on vacation. So far we've seen Georgetown in Washington D.C., University of South Florida near Tampa, Boise State in Idaho, Columbia and NYU in New York City and the University of Michigan in Ann

Arbor. In past trips to Texas, we've been through Texas A&M, Rice and University of Texas in Austin. Then there were tours of Fresno State, Cal State Northridge, UCLA, Pepperdine, San Diego State, UCSD and University of San Diego during numerous adventures in Southern Cal. We've even done day trips to CAL, Stanford and UC Davis locally. Sadly, we missed Oxford when in England last year, but knowing they don't have much of a football program it probably wouldn't have made our short list. Needless to say, we're well stocked when it comes to hoodies, t-shirts and flannel loungewear with college logos.

I'm going to tour Ohio State. **Conner B., MVHS Class of 2016**

When planning to visit a college or university it's best to book a tour in advance. The traditional campus walking tour usually takes about ninety minutes and begins in the university administration building or student union. In most cases, a student volunteer will lead the tour and answer questions. It's a chance for high school students to view the school's various academic and athletic facilities, observe classes and experience campus life from the safe confines of an organized group. It's a lot like a safari jeep ride through a wild animal park. Somehow every tour ends at the student bookstore. Truthfully, the best part of a prospective college campus tour may be the quality time parents get to spend with their children. As self-assured as your high school junior may seem at home, most are a little overwhelmed when walking a college campus for the first time.

I want to visit my dad's alma mater, Stanford, as well as the Ivy League schools (Princeton, Yale and Harvard). **Conner S., SRVHS Class of 2016**

Interestingly enough, a lot of kids will have a tough time getting into their first-choice colleges. From what we've seen, the UC system requires an 8.0 GPA and a perfect 2400 SAT score (plus ace the extra credit questions) to be worthy of consideration. At the same time, there are some highly desirable out of state schools where acceptance is just as tough. My guess is colleges in Minnesota might be the exception, where seven of the top ten coldest weather college campuses are located. The University of Minnesota - Morehead (Ranked #1 coldest campus) might consider eliminating academic requirements for California kids altogether as an incentive to increase applications. Unless I'm mistaken, their brochure tag line reads, "Just pack warm clothes."

I'm looking forward to touring Pepperdine, Cal Poly SLO, USC and Chapman. **Jasmine D., MVHS Class of 2016**

My friends and I agree that most of us would have trouble finding a college that would accept us (outside of the Minnesota schools) given our mediocre high school grades. I'm happy to report that kids today take their high school studies so much more seriously due in large part to the competitive nature of college admissions. If memory serves me, the toughest class I had my junior year was an English class where we read such tame literary masterpieces as *The Count of Monte Cristo* and *The Scarlet Letter*. Unless I'm mistaken my daughter's class is currently reading *War & Peace*, the Bible (for literary purposes) and the collective works of Will Shakespeare. Math and sciences were my scholastic kryptonite. I may have stumbled through Algebra I and Geometry, but I truly had to grovel for a passing grade in Biology. My little girl is already trudging through chemistry and Algebra II. I knew my collegiate future was going to be at the local community college (Foothill JC) followed by a state school (CSU Northridge), so in my mind there was no point in pushing myself. Given the choice between trigonometry and photography, taking pictures won every time. Sadly, film developing is a lost art. It's not uncommon for today's high school junior to be a student athlete, enrolled in several AP classes, a member of a school club and involved in at least one community service project.

I can't wait to visit Scripps Institute at UC San Diego. **Ally A., SRVHS Class of 2016**

My wife and I encourage our high school junior daughter to think big and we want her to attend the college of their choice (within reason), but that means buckling down with her studies. Allow me to say, I am crazy proud of how hard both my girls work to bring home good grades. To say I'm a little envious about their future is an understatement. To be a high school junior with a world of opportunities in front of you would be surreal. I try and explain to my daughter that it's different in other parts of the bay area, state and country, where economics play a significant part in your advanced education opportunities, but along the I-680 corridor, attending college is a forgone conclusion.

I never even visited Fresno State before committing to go to school there. It was close enough to home for my parents not to object and it had the major I wanted. **Julie C., Marina High School Class of 1979**

4 The Allure of High School Graduation

When one thinks of June, we undoubtedly conjure up images of all the beautiful and talented women, past and present, named June: country singer June Carter-Cash, actress June Lockhart, Model June Wilkinson, Pointer Sister June Pointer, the Beaver's mom June Cleaver and reality star Mama June Shannon (Honey Boo-Boo's beloved mother). Come to think of it, football coach June Jones might be more attractive and beloved than Mama June. He's certainly more refined, but that's just one man's opinion.

The calendar month of June, on the other hand, is synonymous with many glorious events including weddings, vacations and graduations. As families all along the I-680 Corridor prepare for high school graduation, on or around Friday June 10th, there's not a house, condo or townhome that will not be experiencing high levels of excitement, giddiness and euphoria. Once Senior Ball, Declare Day and final exams are completed, the days leading up to the actual commencement ceremony are a magical time consisting of yearbook signing, pool parties, and mani/pedis. That countdown to "Grad" day has begun. Grad Day is the culmination of K-12 schooling that signals an end to the monotonous school rules, rituals, routines, homework and horrible cafeteria food.

Whether your high school senior is headed to college, trade school or the military, they are on their way to their future. But first, they must go through the cap and gown ceremony, grad night and a few dozen Beer Pong-themed grad parties. At my high school graduation ceremony, I couldn't wait to be released from the shackles of education and be free of high school. Granted, I did attend a boys' detention center where we did actually wear shackles under our robes, so this was a literal reference, not just a figurative one. I had to know the difference between literal and figurative to get my GED diploma, but I digress. Graduation is a special time for any teenager and one that will be a lifelong memory. If you're interested, I have a few other "graduation" thoughts and memories.

The movie *The Graduate* was a film released in 1967 that tells the story of a disillusioned college graduate (Dustin Hoffman) who's torn between his older lover (Anne Bancroft) and her daughter (Katherine Ross). I do remember watching that movie for the first time while I was in high school, and just wishing I had Ben Braddock's (Hoffman's character) dilemma. At my high school there were several girls who had very attractive mothers that fell into that "WOW" category. I won't name names, Donna Granowski, but I ran *The Graduate* movie in my head too many times to count with one Mrs. Granowski playing the part of the alluring and seductive Mrs. Robinson. Sorry Donna.

I'm not a big fan of Kanye West, the celebrity, but before he became Mr. Kardashian he released a CD entitled *Graduation* that was brilliant. I'm here to tell you, *Graduation* is an amazing collection of boldly crafted songs by an incredibly talented master wordsmith. Very few of my countless number of fans know that I love me some hip-hop. Truth be told, I have actually counted all of my fans and I'm up to seventeen. Kanye's third studio album was released in September of 2007. The CD contained numerous bold, innovative and utterly captivating lyrical masterpieces such as: "Stronger," "Good Life, Good Morning," "The Glory," and "Everything I Am." Kanye won his third Grammy when *Graduation* was named Best Rap Album. Some might say that with the *Graduation* album, Kayne graduated to a larger pop culture acceptance and audience (this was all before he became the circus clown he is today.)

Sadly, the high school graduation episode of most teen television series often proves to be the kiss of death for many of the main characters and decent plot lines, beginning with *Happy Days,* which aired in 1977 and revealed Fonzie's secret plan to graduate with Ritchie and Potsy's senior class. You can't have a town hoodlum go all cap and gown. What were they thinking? Different story lines, but the same results followed *Saved by the Bell, The Wonder Years, Boy Meets World, Beverly Hills 90210,* all the way up to *Glee's* graduation episode in 2012. Did anyone really think Finn and Rachel would get married when she had a chance to star on Broadway? Come on! It seems that graduation day is usually when a good teen series "jumps the shark" and begins its downward descent. While the series regulars always seem so youthful, enthusiastic and filled with promise while in high school, the minute they graduate they appear awkwardly older, directionless and seemingly out of place. It goes totally off the rails when these 18-20 year-old college dropouts pursue unrealistic careers like club owner, apparel designer and politician.

Graduation itself starts with the procession of academic staff and students. The school band will likely play some off-key version of the graduation walking song, "Pomp and Circumstance" to get everyone's attention. The principal or school superintendent will wax on, trying to inspire the 2016 class to greatness. The class valedictorian will try his or her best not to throw up or wet themselves. Someone (often times the school janitor) will eventually get around to handing out the diplomas. The ceremony ends with caps being thrown in the air and Facebook blowing up as proud parents post millions of iPhone images of their kid's noteworthy accomplishment. Let me stop now before I start tearing up. That darn pollen.

This year, as we sit through the commencement address, invocation and speeches, try and recall your own graduation ceremony and see what kind of memories it brings back. What type of hopes and dreams did you have on that special day? I envy where the kids are today, but they are also faced with challenges much different than anything we ever had to consider. The good news is the possibilities are limitless once they graduate... college. Check back with me in four years.

Making a Difference by Volunteering

I have frequently preached from my magazine pulpit about the joys and benefits of volunteering and community service. To volunteer is to perform or give services of your own free will, to assume an obligation voluntarily. The benefits of volunteerism are numerous and yet the rewards are usually very personal.

"I volunteer my time as a way to give back to my community. I find it personally fulfilling to dedicate my time and energy to a cause I believe in that benefits those in need." —Anonymous.

Margaret Mead once said, "Never doubt that a small group of thoughtful, committed citizens can change the world, indeed, it's the only thing that ever has." The Thrift Station in downtown Danville exemplified this ideal perfectly. The Thrift Station is staffed only by a volunteer auxiliary known affectionately as "The Friends of Discovery." That would be Discovery Counseling Center of San Ramon Valley and the proceeds from The Thrift Station play a vital role in supporting mental health care in our community.

Friends of Discovery was established in 1972 by Marge Early. With 35 volunteers they opened the first Thrift Station store in April of 1973. After several moves, they settled in their current location in 2004 and today there are over 140 dedicated volunteers. Last spring, The Thrift Station celebrated their 45th anniversary and over the years they have accumulated an impressive collection of community service awards including being named the Danville Area Chamber of Commerce Non Profit Business of the Year. Jenise Falk, a former principal with the San Ramon Valley Unified School District, is now the President of the Friends of Discovery. Janise praises the team of volunteers at The Thrift Station for their tireless dedication to a worthwhile cause. "These wonderful women (and a few men) devote themselves to a cause they believe in and their efforts truly make a difference in this area."

"Only a life lived for others is a life worthwhile." —Albert Einstein

The Alameda Country Community Food Bank in Oakland is another wonderful volunteer cause. ACCFB has stood by the unwavering belief that food is a basic human right. They distribute millions of meals every year and are on the forefront of a new approach to ending hunger and poverty. Nearly 17,000 volunteers put in over 103,000 hours every year help to ensure that children, adults and seniors in Alameda County know where their next meal will come from. Five (sometimes six) days a week, their warehouse and office are a buzz with volunteer activity. Whether packing food in the warehouse, staffing the Emergency Food Helpline or assisting in the office with events and other projects, volunteer contribution is a critical part of the food bank's efforts.

"We couldn't feed the community without the help of our volunteers to sort and package, bag and deliver to our clients, which are 1 in 5 county residents. It's incredible to see how much can be accomplished by a group of volunteers in just a 2-3 hour shift. What our volunteers do improves the lives of those who receive it," says Michael Altfest, Director of Community Engagement & Marketing, Alameda County Community Food Bank. Check out their website at www.accfb.org.

Meals on Wheels provides a network of services that allow seniors to live in their home with dignity and independence and another local volunteer opportunity within the community. Volunteer Cathy Tisa says, "I get a sense of real purpose working with seniors who are on a tight budget, have limited mobility and truly appreciate kindness and conversation." www.mowsf.org

"The only ones among us who will be truly happy are those who have sought and found how to serve." —Albert Schweitzer

Kids Against Hunger is an all-volunteer organization focused on feeding families around the world and around the corner. Last fall, the San Ramon Valley Thunderbirds varsity football team worked a shift at the Pleasanton facility. The players and coaches filled bags with a fortified soy/rice casserole style meal specifically formulated to meet the nutritional needs of starving children. Head Coach Sean Gann thought this would be an eye-opening teamwork experience for his young team made of primarily eighth-grade boys from the greater Danville area. Most walked away with a stronger sense of appreciation after hearing how their two-hour shift would benefit so many families with kids their age. For more information contact www.kahbayarea.org.

"We make a living by what we get, but we make a life by what we give." —Winston Churchill

A wonderful outdoor activity can be found with The East Bay Regional Parks District, which runs a volunteer trail maintenance program each year that extends from April through November and includes approximately eight separate projects throughout the East Bay. The volunteers typically work from 8:30 am to 1:00 pm on a scenic East Bay park creating new hiking paths, eliminating brush and debris or eliminating an old trail that had become obsolete and troublesome. Check out their website at www.ebparks.org.

Volunteering in our community is one of the most rewarding and enriching experiences we can share. You typically meet a variety of people performing the duties at hand for a menagerie of fulfilling reasons. People often walk away with a renewed sense of appreciation, empathy and compassion. I encourage everyone to give some form of volunteering a try because the lives it changes might start with your own.

6 Dadisms

I have been a dad for almost twenty years. Despite what you might have heard to the contrary from two Danville girls in their late teens whose names rhyme with Banana and Bear, I'd like to think I'm a pretty good dad. There's no question I have a few flaws—over protective, overly involved and I like my eggs over easy—however, I try my best to overcompensate for my weaknesses by not being hypocritical or judgmental. Instead, I've always tried to be patient, understanding, compassionate, empathetic, and loving. Like every father/daughter relationship, we have our share of arguments, disagreements and general conflict, but there are alot more good days than bad, (roughly a 29:1 ratio most months). If you're the emotional type and cry easily, feel free to pause and grab a tissue before continuing with the rest of this article. You see, the two greatest days of my roughly 19,692 days on earth were the days Hannah and Claire were born, followed closely by the day I made First-Team All-League my senior year of high school football. But seriously, I truly love being a dad and the time I get to spend with these two smart, funny, beautiful, creative, clever, compassionate, strong, amazing young women.

In past articles, I've declared that being a dad is the greatest job in the world, but in reality, being a dad isn't a job at all. There's no pay, no regular hours and no personal time off or paid vacation. The dad job doesn't offer stock options, a 401K or even an expense account. Despite the fact that I am the family CEO, I don't get any of the fancy CEO perks like a car allowance, Giants season tickets or even my own designated parking stall. No, being a dad is more a life choice and the greatest choice I've ever made. The joy is immeasurable.

It's been a big "DAD" adjustment with Hannah being away

at the University of Colorado and now, with Claire getting ready to attend the University of Oklahoma in the fall. I fear coming to grips with the reality of "empty nest syndrome" will be more difficult than once imagined. Where are my tissues?

As a dad, part of my "job" description includes inspiring and lifting up my children whenever possible. Ever since my girls were presented with a Danville-required smart phone, immediately following their fifth grade promotion ceremony, I have sent them periodic text messages that I thought were profound, topical, motivational, encouraging and, dare I say, inspirational. I come across these jewels in books, songs, and my friends' Facebook posts. Occasionally, I make one up. I like to call them <u>Dadisms</u>. Please allow me to share a sampling of my Dadisms with you now. Again, keep the tissues close.

If you can't be good, be careful.

Forget all the reasons why it won't work and believe the one reason why it will.

Pay attention to your gut feelings. No matter how good something looks, if it doesn't feel right....walk away.

Be nice to someone for no reason. You never know when you'll need someone to be nice to you.

Success seems to be connected with action. Successful people keep moving. They make mistakes, but they don't give up.

Be somebody who makes everybody feel like somebody.

Don't chase people. Be an example. Attract them. The people who belong in your life will come find you and stay. Just be yourself and do your thing.

A person who feels appreciated will always do more than what is expected.

When you see something beautiful in someone, tell them! It may take seconds to say, but for them, it could last a lifetime.

If someone treats you like crap, just remember that there's something wrong with them, not you. Don't go around destroying other people.

Think before you speak. Is it true, is it helpful, is it inspiring, is it necessary and is it kind?

Who to spend time with: Those who make you better, those who want to see you grow, those who see the greatness in you, those who are good for your mental health, those who are inspired, excited and grateful and those who force you to push yourself up a level

Don't be impressed by: money, followers, degrees and titles. Be impressed by: kindness, integrity, humility and generosity.

Rules of Action: If you do not go after what you want, you will never get it. If you do not ask, the answer will always be "NO". If you do not step forward, you will always be in the same place.

Family isn't always blood. It's the people in your life who want you in theirs; the ones who accept you for who you are. The ones who would do anything to see you smile and who love you no matter what.

Beauty isn't about having a pretty face, it's about having a kind heart, an accepting mind and a beautiful soul.

We don't grow when things are easy we grow when we face challenges.

Life lessons are rarely inexpensive or painless.

Good friends are like stars. You don't always see them, but you know they're always there.

If you stumble, make it part of the dance.

There comes a time in your life, when you walk away from all the drama and people who create it. You surround yourself with people who make you laugh. Forget the bad and focus on the good. Love the people who treat you right and pray for the ones who don't. Life it too short to be anything but happy.

10 Things that require zero talent: Being on time, work ethic, body language, a positive attitude, passion, being coachable, effort, extra effort, being prepared and listening.

Take pride in how far you've come and have faith in how far you can go.

You either get better or you get bitter. It's that simple. You either deal with what life has dealt you and allow it to make you a better person or you allow it to tear you down. The choice does not belong to fate, it belongs to you.

Having real friends is better than having many friends.

Successful people build each other up. They motivate, inspire and encourage each other. Unsuccessful people just hate, blame and complain.

No matter how educated, rich or cool you believe you are, how you treat people tells all. Integrity is everything.

Pick your battles. Sometimes peace is better than being right.

Other ways to say "I love you"...I miss you, sweet dreams, Are you hungry? How's your day going? Drive careful, Call me when you get there so I know you're safe, I hope you're feeling better, Be careful, Don't worry - I'll take care of it for you, Do you need a hug? You don't have to hear the words "I love you" to know you're loved. Listen carefully, people speak from the heart in more ways than one.

Do not think of today's failures, but of the success that may come tomorrow. You have set yourself a difficult task, but you will succeed. If you persevere, you will find joy in overcoming obstacles.

Life is amazing and then it's awful, and then it's amazing again. In between amazing and awful it's ordinary and mundane and routine. Breathe in the amazing, hold on through the awful and relax and exhale during the ordinary. That's just living our heartbreaking, healing, amazing, awful, ordinary lives and it's heartbreakingly beautiful.

Sometimes all you need is twenty seconds of insane courage. Just literally twenty seconds of simple embarrassing bravery and I promise you something great can come of it.

There are more, but I don't want to lose my audience. For those of you still awake, I hope you have enjoyed this glimpse into my sensitive dad soul. When I'm not being deep, I occasionally send something light-hearted such as this gem: I often look at my children and can't see me in them. Then they open their mouth and say something sarcastic and I'm like...oh, there I am. If you think your son or daughter could benefit from receiving one of these nuggets above, please feel free to pass along your own Dadism or Momism.

With the house soon to be very quiet, I may finally have to find a hobby that pays more than writing magazine articles. Perhaps I'll create my own Dadisms App. I've already got the copyright *#dadisms* and the domain name….. www.dadisms.com. Don't forget Father's Day is June 18th.

7 College Kids and Parents Weekend
Rejuvenating and Expensive

We recently returned from Parents Weekend (aka Family Weekend) at the University of Colorado, Boulder ("Sko Buffs") where we visited our eldest daughter, Hannah. In a few weeks, we'll be jetting off to Norman, Oklahoma for Parents Weekend at the University of Oklahoma ("Boomer Sooner"). Parents Weekend is the ideal time for my baby momma and I to visit our girls in their natural collegiate habitat, to rejuvenate the family bond and to confirm that they're both still enrolled. Parents Weekend is heartwarming, fun, chaotic, eye opening, expensive and exhausting, especially for the freshman parents going through it for the first time.

This was our third Parents Weekend at CU and it will be our second at OU. I'm impressed with the schools that realize freshman and sophomores, and to some degree even upperclassmen, need a little family loving 5-7 weeks into the fall semester. It's also a great opportunity to sell a lot of school merch and swag. Typical Parents Weekends are action-packed, with planned activities on or around campus (tours, tailgates and a home football game) and the family activities off campus, usually involving a credit card (shopping, lunch, shopping, dinner, shopping, housekeeping/cleaning and more shopping). Our credit cards are as tired as we are after these whirlwind weekends.

Planning for Parents Weekend starts with booking flights. Unless you're lucky enough to have your kids attend one of the many California colleges or universities within driving distance, Southwest will likely get you virtually anywhere else, on time and in one piece, for a price. Flying isn't cheap unless you're willing to take a few scheduling and safety risks on some of the economy airlines, (rhymes with Fearit and Brontier). Once you secure travel, it's time to book your accommodations. Unless I'm mistaken, every hotel, motel, plaza and inn located anywhere near a college or university chooses the four times a year to really jack up the room rates. Those would logically be move-in weekend, move-out weekend, Homecoming weekend and Parents Weekend. A word to the wise, unless you book a room close to a year in advance, you'll likely be staying in the next city, county or state. The last part of your Parents Weekend travel plans involves renting a car. Most rent-a-car companies aren't logged into the same "gouge the college parent consumer" chat room as the hotels, but it's just one more expense. Just for the record, we like Alamo.

Once Mom and Dad (siblings are optional) arrive somewhere near campus (dorm, student housing, fraternity/sorority house or off-campus residence) on Friday, the first order of business is a meal. Most of our kids are so sick of their normal food options they are dying for a good meal, one that they don't have to pay for or Super Size. That's usually followed by a trip to CVS, Safeway, Costco, Walmart and/or Sam's Club. Kids need stuff. Stuff includes groceries, toiletries, clothes, school supplies, accessories, coffee, cleaning supplies and knick-knacks. Individually, nothing is tremendously pricey, but collectively it can all easily add up to a week's worth of wages or more.

Shopping is followed by a visit to your child's living pod where you immediately realize that despite how clean and tidy the family home is kept, most college kids live in filth and squalor. Apparently, not one of our sweet, loveable, capable, manageable, knowledgeable spawn can keep a clean room. It must be a right of passage, but as parents, a lot of us can't help but break out into "clean-mode." It's not like we're going to break out the fire hose and five-gallon drum of Scrubbing Bubbles, but we're going to sweep, vacuum or wipe before the toxic mold spreads.

Friday night concludes with a casual dinner followed by coffee or dessert. It's really nice if you run into some of your kid's new friends and can ask a series of canned and rehearsed questions. 1. Where are you from? 2. How did you two meet? 3. What are you studying? 4. Do you like your roommates? 5. Are these your parents or probation officers? Then it's time to get back to the hotel to rest up for game day. That is, unless your child attends a football-less institution, in which case I don't know what you would do on Saturday. Flea market, craft fair or sports bar perhaps?

Parents Weekend has been an amazing experience for me! I have two students at the same school and I really look forward to Parents Weekend each year. It gives me the chance to see my kids in their own environment, interacting with their friends. I can share in the fun of watching competitive football, and socialize with other students' parents at various tailgate parties. The college years are going by way too fast. Parents Weekend has given me the opportunity to share a part of my kid's life journey with them. Cara V.

Saturday is all about the game, along with the pregame and postgame activities. My girls like to tailgate. Fraternity tailgates are a $h*t Show. Cheap warm beer, ear-splitting loud music and disgusting bathrooms are all part of the charming ambiance leading up to kick-off. Sadly, fraternities apparently don't have a budget for hotdogs. Few sporting events are as much fun as college football games. Marching bands, cheerleaders, mascots, alumni, home field advantage and school spirit are part of the sensory overload. The game is the game, but it's always fun just being there for an average price of $90 per ticket. Postgame is usually code for "let's go out to a nice dinner this time." Following a pricey meal, the kiddies are likely going to float from party to party on a Saturday night which means they'll dismiss us back to our hotel at a reasonable hour. Fortunately, most hotel bars are filled with parents, still wearing their bookstore-purchased apparel, stopping for a nightcap. This is a nice time to network and commiserate.

Sunday starts with breakfast or brunch…. somewhere. At CU it's the sorority and at OU it's one of the 273 *Jimmy's Egg* restaurants in the state of Oklahoma. This is the weekend wrap-up before parents head home via highway or byway, aka airports. We tell the kids to study hard, get plenty of rest, take care of themselves and have fun, but not too much fun. "If you can't be good, be careful" is my signature Dad line. There are usually a few tears (mostly mine) as we say our goodbyes, but knowing that they'll be home soon enough for Thanksgiving is our saving grace.

Truth be told, Parents Weekend is the perfect opportunity to recharge the parent and child emotional batteries and at the end of the weekend we couldn't care less how much it costs. That's what home equity loans are for, right?

8 Savor the Moments

We've all had our moments. Good moments and bad moments, happy moments and sad moments, moments of triumph and moments of failure. I, for one, have had moments that I'm extremely proud of and moments that have caused me great embarrassment. HUGE embarrassment. I'm pretty sure I wet myself in the outfield of my first Pee Wee league baseball game and then again when I over-drank at a brothers only fraternity retreat. Not my proudest moments. Let's face it, we've all shared "moments" with friends, relatives, neighbors, co-workers, classmates, casual acquaintances and complete strangers. Moments that vary on the emotional Richter scale from regrettable to forgettable to absolutely remarkable. A positive moment (a first kiss), might be something we reflect on for a lifetime while a negative moment (falling asleep at a wedding ceremony – just as an example) might be something to bury in the past forever.

Recently while watching my favorite "guilty pleasure" television series, *This Is Us*, I could totally relate when Rebecca, trying to make sense of her dysfunctional mother-son relationship with Kevin, said, "It wasn't all bad. We had our moments. I feel it in my soul, we had some really good moments." Yes, I choked up, I'm sensitive that way. I own it. Given that my own daughters have struggled with a strained relationship for most of their teenage years, I had just told each of them, individually the day before, "it hasn't all been bad, you've had some moments that were good and fun." This obviously explains the reason for the mistiness in my eyes that particular Tuesday evening around 9:55.

Sibling Moments: As a brother with three sisters, I've shared a million moments, both good and bad, with these three she-devils. At any given time over the last fifty years, at least one of them hasn't been talking to me. We have shared sad and happy moments when we cried at each of our parent's funerals and celebrated at all of our children's births. We've also laughed at crazy, funny, silly moments that only siblings get or can relate to. However, my favorite moments were fleeting conversations that were both deeply personal and genuinely heartfelt. The type of conversation that only a brother and sister can appreciate . . . even when they're not talking years later.

When I asked my daughters what their special moments together were, they talked about playing Barbies for hours on rainy days, the joy as they walked into an American Girl Doll store for the first time, the excitement of seeing Santa placing gifts under the tree on Christmas Eve and a spontaneous Sunday afternoon at a Giants game. See, despite a lot of nasty fights, they have had their sweet and positive moments.

Parenting Moments: The tender, loving, magical moments of being a parent are like nothing else. It starts with the moment you first hold your newborn baby. Life-changing will forever be an understatement. I loved the moments of stand-rocking my babies to sleep while listening to a Marc Cohn or Kenny Loggins CDs. Don't judge. Developmental moments such as first steps, first words, potty training or riding a bike are hard to describe unless you've been there to experience them firsthand. What are just as momentous are times of sadness, emotion, sorrow, frustration and heartbreak that can be difficult and painful, but all part of the parenting experience. The moment I became a father was the greatest moment of my life, twice.

Parented Moments: My dad was a twenty-four-year U.S. Navy veteran, born and bred in the South. Although he was a man of few words, we had our moments. The teaching me to drive moment or the fishing and shooting guns back in Texas moments are irreplaceable. Anytime I felt I made him proud of me was a moment that's hard for a son to describe in writing.

My mom on the other hand was a "moment machine," always encouraging, supporting and willing me to succeed in school, sports, downright everything. Sadly, because they both passed away so young, all I have are those deeply personal moment memories to hold on to and pass along to my kids.

Marriage Moments: Asking someone to marry you is a nerve-wracking, sweat generating moment, as is the actual marriage ceremony. Finding out you're going to have a baby and then actually having one (or more) is a life-altering moment. Married couples have plenty of moments, some bigger than others and not all easy ones to navigate, but every marriage is full of them.

Sports Moments: Sporting moments, aka "Glory Days" often stay with us forever. We can tell you about a Little League home run hit forty-five years ago like it was yesterday. I hit three my twelve-year-old year for whatever it's worth. I've written about certain gridiron moments from high school or college that helped define me as a player and as a person. The moment I crossed the finish line at the 2011 Chicago Marathon puts an immediate smile on my face, knowing what went into accomplishing that moment. There is always a lot of determination mixed with sweat and countless hours dedicated to any serious athletic endeavor; however, those irreplaceable moments that will last a lifetime override all the pain and agony.

Work Moments: Work is work, but I've had a few moments as a commission salesman that were memorable. Closing that first deal, closing that huge deal or closing that brain damaged difficult deal were all moments. Leaving one company and starting with another is a cautiously optimistic/nervous excitement moment. Often times, it's the people we work with that help up create a moment and for some reason that makes me think of the brilliant television sitcom, *The Office*.

Valentine's Day Moments: I'm no Don Juan, but I've had my romantic moments. In third grade, I gave Kelly Mullford a plagiarized poem, passing it off as my own. Sadly, Dr. Seuss has a certain, easy to identify style to his writing. In my early twenties, I had my girlfriend wait just inside Macy's in San Francisco while I ran to get the car during a torrential downpour. Along the way, I stopped to buy her a bunch of flowers from a street vendor. I was drenched when I picked her up, but the gesture won me mooches smooches. As a husband and father of daughters, my feel-good moment was seeing my wife and little girls faces light up when the florist annually delivered flowers to all three of them on Valentine's Day.

Moments are just that, a moment in time that has a lasting impact on us. A moment can occur in an instant, jiffy or flash. It can last seconds, minutes or hours. There really is no defined duration that constitutes a moment. While it can be fleeting, it can also be immeasurable as a lasting moment forever burned into your heart and mind. The key is to never stop trying to create a moment for yourself or someone else. While an article I wrote a few years ago encouraged my readers to appreciate the small things, I'm now here to tell you, savor the moments.

III

Holiday Madness

The holidays, as a topic, is easy game for this hunter. Christmas and Hanukkah, Thanksgiving, Halloween, New Year's, St. Valentine's Day, Easter/Passover and Super Bowl Sunday are all holidays that I enjoy writing about for the magazine. Who can't relate to crass commercialization, annoying relatives, unappreciative children, mass consumption of food and alcohol and television programming?

1 Finding the Holiday Spirit

Truth be told, as an empty nester, I find it difficult to get into the holiday spirit without listening to my Harry Connick Jr. Christmas CD while sipping on a little eggnog Moscow Mule holiday liquid cheer, if you know what I mean? Unless you have small children in your home or a workshop full of elves, maybe a reindeer or two, the holiday spirit can be a bit hard to come by for us grown-ups.

Here is my Top 10 list of activities and outings to put yourself in the holiday spirit or drive yourself to the brink of Mistletoe Madness. It could go either way.

10. Holiday Shows. Watching one of the thousands of holiday movies or television programs can really kick off the holiday season. Who doesn't enjoy their 50th viewing of *Santa Claus is Coming to Town, Frosty the Snowman, Rudolph the Red-Nose Reindeer, Elf, It's a Wonderful Life, A Christmas Carol, The Grinch Who Stole Christmas, Little Drummer Boy, A Charlie Brown Christmas, The Santa Clause (1, 2 & 3), The Polar Express, Home Alone, Bad Santa, Shrek the Halls*, NBC's Tree Lighting from Rockefeller Center and every cheesy holiday movie on the Hallmark Channel from November 1st through New Year's Day. I especially enjoy stringing cranberries while I watch my holiday shows (NOT), but a little liquid cheer will add to the holiday spirit.

9. Ice skating (outdoors). There isn't enough peppermint fudge in this world to get me to ice skate at my age, I've got bills to pay and I don't mean medical bills. I can't afford to be laid up for a couple of months with a broken ankle or bruised glute muscle. However, going to an outdoor skating rink to watch other people fall down on the cement-hard ice is a lot of fun. The music, the merriment and the cool crisp air can set a joyful mood. Cups of warm cocoa or cider, with a little liquid cheer, will certainly add to the holiday spirit.

8. Caroling. Organizing a neighborhood caroling cavalcade is a dandy way to get into the spirit of the holiday. What's a cavalcade? It's a procession. Work with me, people. It's safe to say, we all know most of the words to every holiday song; "Jingle Bells," "Oh Come All Ye Faithful," "Deck the Halls," "Rudolph the Red-Nosed Reindeer," "Frosty the Snowman," "Silent Night," "Santa Claus is Coming to Town," "Oh Holy Night," "Hells Bells," (just kidding, that's my favorite AC/DC song) and "Joy to the World." Dress warm, wear sensible shoes and bring along a little liquid cheer to enliven the holiday spirit.

7. Baking. Nothing says holidays more than a house wafting with the delightful odor coming from an oven full of homemade cookies, pumpkin bread, peppermint bark, fudge, biscotti, or a life-sized gingerbread house. It certainly helps mask the offensive odor wafting from a backed-up bathroom following a toilet clogging relative's annual visit. If nothing else, invest in the new Febreze holiday baking scent. A little liquid cheer will undoubtedly add to the holiday spirit and baking creativity.

6. Decorating (indoors). Deck the halls, baby. I'm not saying that everyone's indoor holiday decorating needs to be over the top, but how about getting in the spirit with a few twinkling lights and shiny ornaments on a tree or bush for starters? From there do as little or as much as your heart desires. Personally, I like pasting copy paper scissor-cut icicles on the windows and dangling mistletoe over every arch or doorway, but that's just me. I find that a little liquid cheer will add to the holiday spirit.

5. Decorating (outdoors). Regardless if you live in a house, apartment, townhouse, condo, mobile home or tent, deck the yard, baby. Assuming you follow HOA guidelines, string your lights, arrange a nativity scene and plug in your blow-ups to create an outdoor winter wonderland. Electricity and ladders don't always mix well with libations—trust me, I know—so maybe wait until your Griswold Holiday Vacation light display is completed until you enjoy a little liquid cheer which will add to the holiday spirit.

If you really want to experience a little light bulb envy, visit the Vista San Ramon sub-division in San Ramon (across from Central Park) or the house at 108 Dana Highlands Court in Danville (Woodranch sub-division). I'm pretty sure Santa sees those two locations from 30,000 feet up when he's dropping into the Bay Area on Christmas Eve. I also bet they get a really special holiday card from PG&E every year.

4. Holiday Cards. Addressing and mailing your holiday cards to friends and family is another annual tradition. Due in large part to Shutterfly's brilliant guilt-focused marketing campaign, personal photo cards long ago overtook the popularity of traditional Hallmark cards with a Thomas Kinkade image. Part of the holiday merriment is trying to coordinate an acceptable family photo even if your family simply consists of you and your turtle. Once you have that perfect Kodak moment image, complete with clever saying such as "From our home to yours," addressing the envelopes can take longer than the 12 days of Christmas. As for the envelope, I like to go with a seasonal postage stamp and the cutesy holiday return address stickers that come in every fundraising request envelope I've received the year before. A little liquid cheer will add to the holiday spirit and deaden the envelope licking aftertaste.

3. Visiting Santa Claus. I haven't sat on Santa's lap since I was seven or eight…..teen, but if you really want to get in the spirit, plan a visit to Stoneridge Mall or Broadway Plaza to chat with the jolly, white bearded, present granter (or some reasonable likeness). Let's assume, for argument's sake, you're taking your kids or grandkids, or someone's kids – hopefully with their permission—to also get a photo with Kris Kringle. For only $99.99, you can get a complete picture set, ornament and mug of someone either crying or screaming. Don't laugh, it might be you. I don't recommend that you add liquid cheer to this event as a public intoxication charge or DUI could really dampen the holiday spirit for everyone.

    2. White Elephant Gift Exchange. It doesn't matter if it's your office mates, friends, family, neighbors or cell block, a white elephant gift exchange is almost always fun and festive. That is, unless someone gives you an actual white elephant because those albino pachyderms can really trash your backyard. Having a theme to your gift exchange can add to the shenanigans, but let's keep it PC for fear of offending the seasonal morality police. Liquid cheer is a wonderful theme because you know what I like to say, a little liquid cheer will add to the holiday spirit.

    And the Number One (#1) way to get into the holiday spirit is to give. Give your time or money to the less fortunate, the sad, the lonely or the hurting. Be a friend, a helper or a listener. Donate to a food bank or Toys for Tots, purchase a pre-packed bag of groceries at Safeway, or find a family in need through a school, church or community group. It is better to give than to receive and there are a lot of homeless or sheltered families with children who could use some assistance. Lending a helping hand in some meaningful way can make everyone's holiday brighter and add to the holiday spirit.

    The holiday spirit is in all of us; it just takes a can opener or cork screw to bring it out of some of us. Hopefully, my Top Ten List of ways to find your holiday spirit will help. If not, start with the liquid cheer, but in moderation, and don't drive. Good tidings to you and yours this holiday season.

A Thanksgiving Day Story

Once upon a time there lived a ruggedly handsome writer man (me) who loved Thanksgiving. He (I) loved everything about the holiday including the food, gathering with family, the food, watching football, the food, time off from work, more food, the lead-in to the Christmas/Hanukkah season, dessert, the holiday television specials and, did I mention the food? Our hero (me again) realized that Thanksgiving is not just a time to give thanks, rejoice and eat, but that's a heck of a good place to start. He/me even enjoyed the history of the holiday. There's a lot people don't know about this marvelous holiday, other than what they learned in elementary school. As a pretend investigative journalist, the following is a brief narrative of the history of my favorite holiday.

The first Thanksgiving Day has been tracked back to the year 1621, when the Pilgrims and Native Americans got together for a raging block party, following the Puritan settlers' first harvest in the New World. This feast lasted three days and was attended by 90 Native Americans and 53 Pilgrims (as accounted by attendee Edward Winslow). I think my high school math teacher may actually have attended as well. The location of the inaugural event was the Plymouth Plantation, located somewhere near Plymouth Rock in Massachusetts. It was reported to be a crisp autumn day with light winds off the Atlantic, or so says www.weatherhistory.com.

Wikipedia doesn't state that the day started out with a scaled-down version of the Macy's Thanksgiving Day Parade, but I did some research. Apparently retired plow horses pulled flat-bed wagons serving as the first floats of the modern era. The blow-up balloon characters (Snoopy, Garfield and the Minions) were just raincoats sewn together which explains the lack of detail and clarity. None of this is probably true, but it makes for a good story and Wikipedia doesn't know everything.

Rumor has it the Pilgrims and Indians played a little touch football before dinner on that lovely fall day. Although technically, the game of football and footballs themselves had not yet been invented, so when it was reported that they threw the old pigskin around, it was an actual dead pig. This obviously explains why the game was originally called Pig Ball. The pilgrims requested to be called the Patriots and the Native American Indians, while technically having red skin, objected to the team name Redskins due to the derogatory term and the political incorrectness of the lame mascot. The warriors and chiefs instead chose Dolphins as their team name because they liked dolphins. The Patriots supposedly won by a field goal probably because they cheated. Look it up at www.pigballhistory.com

Immediately following the game, players from the two teams enjoyed a few libations such as ale and firewater while scarfing down a fine selection of appetizers including chips & dip, raccoon pizza rolls, possum kabobs and a nice cheese platter consisting of smoked gouda, brie, havarti and of course goat cheese.

The dinner itself was legendary. Delicacies included roast turkey with stuffing, cranberry sauce, roasted and sweet potatoes and breads. Local vegetables that likely appeared on the table included onions, corn, squash, various beans, lettuce, spinach, cabbage, carrots and perhaps peas. Seafood dishes might have included lobster, bass, clams, oysters and mussels. The dessert menu assuredly had pumpkin and apple pies, custard, Jello and roasted gourds with a little milk, honey and spices. I love me a good gourd and I found a variety of delectable recipes at www.gourdrecipies.com

There was the obvious post-meal nap for most of the men in attendance as the women folk did the dishes and attended to the children. As the night wound down, the Pilgrims and Indian families likely watched a humorous puppet show or listened to some melodic banjo and harmonica tunes. I like banjo and harmonica music as much as the next guy, just check out my iTunes account (www.hillbillytunes.com), but living in the modern day, my favorite post-food coma activity is watching a good movie. A few movies worth watching on Thanksgiving Day night include *While You Were Sleeping* (with Sandra Bullock), *The Proposal* (with Sandra Bullock) and *Miss Congeniality* (with Benjamin Bratt and Sandra Bullock). You really can't go wrong with any movie staring Sandy B.

After the inaugural meal, this tradition of holding an annual harvest festival didn't firmly take root until the late 1660s. It has been celebrated as a Federal Holiday every year since 1863, when, during the Civil War, President Abraham Lincoln proclaimed a national day of "Thanksgiving and Praise to our beneficent Father who dwelleth in the Heavens." That undoubtedly seemed a little wordy and too religious so somewhere along the line it was taken down to simply a day of "Giving Thanks." In a recent interview, Donald Trump said that it was his idea. The actual "day and date" that we celebrate on has also been somewhat floating, usually taking place sometime in the late October-Mid November time frame. It wasn't until 1941 that President Franklin D. Roosevelt signed a joint resolution of Congress proclaiming the fourth Thursday of November the official day. This likely coincided with schoolkids needing a few days off so their tiny brains didn't explode between Halloween and Christmas.

By the time you read this article, you'll undoubtedly be planning your Thanksgiving Day menu and decorating the house with cornucopias and belt buckle hats. It should be stated that this ruggedly handsome writer and his family don't have any plans and are available to join in a lucky reader's family festivities. We usually go out of town to visit friends during the long holiday weekend, but because of previously scheduled commitments we will be around. What could be more fun than sharing your holiday fun with a guy who loves everything Thanksgiving? It would make a great new chapter in the Thanksgiving Day story.

3 Pass Me the Drumstick

I am a leg man! I love me some legs. What? I am referring to the turkey leg (aka drumstick) when it comes to our Thanksgiving Day entree. Did you think I was going the way of Donald Trump and Billy Bush in a hot mic *Access Hollywood* motorhome conversation? This is a holiday piece for a nice family magazine. I really do like the turkey leg and usually spend most our holiday meal gnawing on the dark meat filled drumsticks like I'm an overweight European Baron from some Elizabethan romance novel. "Serving wench, what do you mean there's no Cool Whip for the pumpkin pie latte? Off with her head!"

I suppose it's more refined to dine on the finely carved white or dark meat of a Tom Turkey, but I'm not some snooty overdressed English Pilgrim trying to hook up with one of the hot looking Native American squaws. I'm all about calorie consumption and a tastebud orgasm. For what it's worth, I also enjoy the drumsticks from the Turkey's less prestigious cousin, the chicken. I was practically raised on fried, baked, barbequed and KFC'd chicken drumsticks. Like my father before me, referenced in last month's article on frugal spending, we like our reasonably priced bird meals. Come to think of it, I believe I've had drumsticks from squab, duck and pheasants to name just a few other edible birds. I've had an ostrich burger at Fuddruckers, but that's one drumstick even beyond my comfort level.

This Thanksgiving Day holiday, a lot of us will be welcoming home our college freshmen for the first time since they departed on their quest for higher education. For most of these kids, it will be the first time sleeping in their beds, arguing with their siblings and adhering to Mom and Dad's rules since they departed for college approximately twelve weeks ago. My independent living collegiate daughter best not have acquired a taste for turkey drumsticks while away at school or she can enjoy her holiday meal at the University Dining Commons. I may extend her curfew and let her sleep in until the crack of noon, but the drumstick thing is non-negotiable. I've heard that it takes both parents and their college freshman children about three months to acclimate to their new life and routine. That's roughly the time period from the start of school at most universities until Thanksgiving break. Their newfound lifestyle does potentially raise some issues when the kids return home and have to follow house rules again and curtail their partying ways. They'll also be driving again and having to avoid all the wild turkeys that populate the greater Mt. Diablo landscape. Trust me, they don't taste nearly as good as a Butterball turkey from Lunardi's in Danville.

By the time this article hits the stands, we'll have elected a new POTUS (President of the United States) with a new FLOTUS (First Lady of the United States) or FHFPOTUS (First Husband Former President). I can only speculate on who won, but what's the point, the American public has likely lost. It doesn't matter if either candidate likes the drumstick or not, they both have so many character flaws that their fowl anatomy choices don't override the scary direction their constant indiscretions may lead our country. As I am a liberal conservative and my wife is a conservative liberal, we usually either agree on a candidate or we cancel out each other's votes. I wish there had been a realistic write-in candidate this year, but neither Condoleezza Rice nor Paul Ryan wanted the job bad enough to give it a go. Well, if nothing else, it gives me, and the equally talented writers at Saturday Night *Live*, plenty of material to work with the next four years.

The month of November is special for more than just Thanksgiving and an occasional insignificant election. This is a month with more going on than most people realize. There's No-Shave November (all month), National Men Make Dinner Day (November 3rd), National Donut Day (November 5th), the official birthday of the U.S. Marine Corps (November 10th), Veteran's Day (November 11th), Mickey Mouse's birthday (November 18th), The anniversary of the Gettysburg Address (November 19th) Black Friday (the last Friday of the month), Small Business Saturday (the last Saturday of the month) and College Football Rivalry Week including: Sunflower Showdown – Kansas vs. Kansas State; Iron Bowl – Auburn vs. Alabama; Civil War – Oregon vs. Oregon State; The Game – Michigan vs. Ohio State (Jim Harbaugh vs. Urban Meyer—should be awesome!); Duel in the Desert – Arizona vs. Arizona State; and The Jeweled Shillelagh – USC vs. Notre Dame. There is so much happening in this mid-to-late fall month that if I didn't have so much leaf raking to do (thanks to the occasional gale-force winds), I might be able to enjoy more than just a delicious drumstick.

Happy Thanksgiving.

They Call Me Mr. Claus

I've always wanted to be a department store Santa. Really, I'm not just saying that for shock value or to shamelessly draw readers into another mind numbing, yet humorous, holiday article. I also don't mean to imply that I want to change careers. However, I think it would be a blast to dress in a Santa suit and get a "boots on the ground" Christmas experience by talking with the true believers at some mall or department store. Are they even still called department stores? Maybe the correct term is now destination shopping experience or multi-level retail goods buying facility. Regardless, Santa is still Santa and I want that gig one day.

In the year 1890, in the small industrial town of Brockton Massachusetts, an American Main Street tradition was born. James Edgar, a philanthropist and department store owner, created a red suit from newspaper sketches and images of St. Nick and made history by becoming America's first department store Santa. Big Jim, as his friends called him, was a tall, heavyset man with a snowy white beard and a booming voice. He opened The Boston Store in Brockton in 1878 and operated the establishment until his death sometime in the early 1900s. He was a happy and prosperous man who loved children. He originally only wore his Santa costume for one hour every afternoon in December, except for Saturdays when he wore it for three hours. He didn't sit on a throne or chair, but instead *wandered* through his store chatting with kids and their parents. Read more about this truly remarkable man at http://firstdepartmentstoresanta.com/yankeemagarticle.pdf

My earliest memories of a department store Santa are from the late 1960s and the Sears and Roebuck store in Mountain View. The Sears Santa, as we called him, was a knock-off Santa.

Cheap Santa suit, lack of padding, less than authentic dreadlocks looking wig and he always smelled of cigarettes and whiskey. Still, believing in old St. Nick at this young age, I couldn't be sure that this wasn't his older (out of work) brother trying to make a little holiday scratch by covering a shift for the big man who was obviously busy managing toy production up at the North Pole. Maybe Santa was just trying to do his bro a solid. Not wanting to take any chances, I treated the man with the respect the office demanded. However, a minor detail always confused me as a snot-nosed elementary school kid. Why, when visiting several stores at one large center or mall (Liberty House, Emporium or Gemco), did each location have their own Santa? Granted, he's magical, but that seemed like a logistical nightmare. Some astute mall manager finally solved this conundrum and somewhere in the late '70s, he or she talked the retail players into pooling their resources and the centrally located Mall Santa was created. Mall Santa came complete with seasonal props, attractive Santa's helpers and a variety of picture package options.

Back in December of 2007, I wrote a delightful holiday piece entitled "A Visit With Santa, the do's and don'ts of a traditional holiday experience." A segment of the article reflected on a place called Santa's Village, which was a Christmas-themed amusement park located off Highway 17 in the heart of the **Santa** Cruz Mountains. During the month of December, this was a festive winter wonderland filled with merriment and holiday magic. The rest of the year it looked like some freaky adult rest stop attracting lonely long-haul truckers, out of work carnies from the **Santa** Cruz Beach Boardwalk, and a lot of pot- growing hempologists hoping to one day see their chosen crop legalized as a pain relieving medicinal alternative. But, alas, I digress. At the height of popularity, Santa's Village was a collection of rides (The Spinning Hot Cocoa Cups), restaurants (Sugar Plum Bistro) and a petting zoo featuring baby reindeer (probably goats). This was department store Santa on steroids. If we were lucky enough to make a pre-Christmas visit, we were convinced that this sit-down on Santa's lap was perhaps the real deal because if this wasn't the real Santa, it was a damn good facsimile. The guy or guys they chose to play the role of Mr. Claus walked the walk and talked the talk. They carried their weight with pride, the hair and beard were authentic (no wigs or weaves) and his naughty/nice list was very convincing. The mountain mirage even employed real life elves, aka dwarfs, midgets (Hmmm... politically incorrect, baldy) ⊚ and/or little people. Even the supposed Mrs. Claus fit the profile perfectly. She rocked her gingerbread apron and bun in a winter bonnet costume. As a family, we only made the pilgrimage to the Soquel Pole once before the property was eventually foreclosed upon. Sadly, some Christmas hating developer bought the land and turned it into a sterile business park on the outskirts of the Silicon Valley. Unless I'm mistaken, they did lease a pad to a fast food operator. My attorney has advised me not to identify the company in print, but let's just say it rhymes with "Fin and Fout Burger." Try the double-double reindeer burger for old time's sake.

The ultimate department store Santa movie is of course *Miracle on 34th Street*. This delightful holiday yarn has been made three separate times. The original version was released in 1947 and starred Edmund Gwenn as Kris Kringle, John Payne, Maureen O'Hara and a very young Natalie Wood. A remake came out in 1973, staring Sebastian Cabot as Santa. Others in the cast included Jane Alexander, David Hartman, Roddy McDowell and Jim Backus. Of the two, I liked seeing Cabot (aka Mr. French) play the bearded-one, however I preferred the original version due to the cinematography of New York City during the mid-1940s. Department stores such as Macy's and Gimbel's were prominent destinations back in the day and Santa had celebrity status. A cheesy television version of the timeless classic was released in 1994 staring Dylan McDermott, Elizabeth Perkins, the precocious Mara Wilson and Sir Richard Attenborough as Father Noel. As much as I was charmed by the adorable Miss Wilson, I couldn't get past Dylan McDermott looking like he wanted to bust into full on Bobby Donnell mode from his hit TV drama, *The Practice*. Elizabeth Perkins has also always creeped me out since she bedded Tom Hanks in the movie *Big*.

I've often wondered if they have a Santa in department stores in other countries. I bet Harrods in London, England would invite Mr. Claus to drop by, but what about Jiuguang in China, Big Bazaar in India or Myer in Australia? I suppose he would be welcome as long as he didn't try to infringe on local customs, sales, religious or cultural traditions. I'll have to keep that in mind if I can't find a department store gig locally. I'm not sure when I'll get a chance to check this Santa experience off my bucket list, but one day I will be channeling my inner Santa sitting on the big chair and sharing the Christmas magic with a line full of holiday crazed kids, hopped up on candy cane dust, anxious to share their list with The Claus Man. "Ho, Ho, Ho!" I need some work on that.

The White Elephant Gift Exchange

At our family White Elephant Gift Exchange this holiday season, I ended up with an actual white elephant. Excuse me, an albino pachyderm, to be more politically correct. I was a little distraught to say the least when my name was drawn last and the only gift still under the menorah tree was a two-ton elephant calf. Who knew someone could actually buy a white elephant for a White Elephant gift exchange? That gift came by way of my out-of-work, over-tattooed, legalize-pot-voting niece which she apparently ordered through Amazon. I thought we had a fifty-dollar limit? Now, in addition to a costly wellness visit to Blackhawk Veterinary, I should probably be expecting a hefty HOA fine next quarter for housing a pet the size of a recreational vehicle in my home.

The folks at Wikipedia tell me the term "white elephant" refers to an extravagant but burdensome gift that cannot be easily disposed of, based on the legend of the King of Siam gifting rare albino elephants to courtiers who had displeased him, that they might be ruined by the animals' upkeep costs. Last year, my White Elephant present was a gift card to Fuddruckers. I love Fuddruckers! What are the chances I can re-gift my elephant between now and Christmas? I do have an office party coming up.

Our family transitioned to a White Elephant gift exchange format after years of going into debt buying presents for every niece/nephew, brother/sister, aunt/ uncle, grandparent, grandchild, step child and second cousin twice removed by a divorce or annulment. I was buying gifts for relatives I never knew I had, assuming they were actually my relatives. I once bought a tie for a guy who was either my half brother-in-law or the young man who delivers our *Contra Costa Times* paper in the morning. Why do we do this? I don't see a lot of these family members except during the holidays and I certainly don't feel overly close to most of them. To be totally honest, I'm more emotionally connected to Hazel in the Costco photo-mat, Rob, a teller at Wells Fargo, and Donna, my favorite checker at Draeger's, than I am to my sister's third boyfriend (following her legal separation) and his five children. Granted, it's the spirit of the season and it's better to give than to receive, but do we need to "give" ourselves into the poorhouse?

I don't want to come off as a more handsome and athletic version of Ebenezer Scrooge; however, it seems to me that families should place more emphasis on connecting throughout the year and not stress so much about what to get each other on this one specific day. I truly don't need any of my friends or relatives spending their hard-earned money on another gift basket from Cost Plus World Market complete with an inexpensive red wine, assorted international cheeses and chocolate covered expresso beans simply out of obligation. It's bad enough that every gift our privileged kids want today is a real-life adaptation of the popular Dr. Suess novel, *The Grinch that Stole My Holiday Paycheck*. There's no such thing as an inexpensive i-anything. Even elephant toys are grossly overpriced.

Getting back to my pachyderm predicament, here are some of my concerns when it comes to raising an elephant in my suburban enclave:

Apparently, elephants love to cuddle. My La-Z-Boy recliner isn't that big or that sturdy.

Apparently, elephants have bad eye site, but a keen sense of smell. Great, I can hide the peanut butter cookies, but he'll probably sniff them out.

Apparently, elephants can live to be seventy years old. That's seventy people years. I'll be lucky if I live to be seventy given that I have an elephant to take care of now.

Apparently, elephants laugh, cry, play and have incredible

memories. So do my neighbor's kids, less the includible memories.

Apparently, elephants love to swim and use their trunks like a snorkel in deep water. What's the leash policy at Oak Hill Park in Danville?

Apparently, elephants are herbivores, spending sixteen hours a day collecting plant food. Their diet is at least 50% grasses, supplemented with leaves, bamboo, twigs, bark, roots, and small amounts of fruits, seeds and flowers. Great, there goes my newly landscaped backyard. If only she just liked an occasional sandwich, our neighborhood has enough wild turkeys and gophers to last her a few years.

Apparently, elephants are one of the few four legged animals who can't run or jump. That must explain the weight issue. Scratch the Frisbee idea.

Apparently, an elephant's trunk has more than 40,000 muscles in it and no bones, which give it the flexibility. However, the trunk can get very heavy at times. So, the elephants are seen to rest it on nearby objects. I better not catch her resting that big old thing on our horribly expensive BBQ Island or she can spell home "S-P-C-A."

If any of my loyal readers thought I actually received a living elephant at a White Elephant holiday gift exchange then we'll have to ask your attendants to take away your paste and crayons for the day. You know how I like to tease. The annual White Elephant family, friends, neighbors, office, club or cellmates gift exchange is a delightful holiday tradition. Sadly, now that I'm finally out of *Alive and Chillin'* books, I may actually have to go out and buy something this year. Maybe I can find a white elephant carved out of actual ivory? Something about that idea doesn't sound ethical, but it's a start. Happy holidays.

6 My Star Wars New Year

January 1st is like a big giant Do-Over for every one of us. No matter how rosy or crappy the previous year was, New Year's Day is our chance to spring out of bed and do it all over again. 365 days of infinite possibilities. Granted, our days aren't all going to be filled with rainbows and unicorns, but hopefully we'll have more good ones than bad. I have decided that my philosophy for the New Year will be heavily influenced by the release of the new Star Wars movie, *The Force Awakens*. Hopefully it will awaken a happy, healthy and prosperous New Year for yours truly.

The seventh installment of the Star Wars franchise or first release of the third trilogy opened on December 18th, 2015. Take this Wookie's word for it, *The Force Awakens* will set every box office revenue record ever recorded in this world or one in a galaxy far far away. Even though we've never met, George Lucas and J.J. Abrams are kind of like my spiritual mentors in this journey so the first thing on my to-do list is to see the movie.

January: Since there's no way any normal person (a non-Star Wars geek) is going to be able to get a ticket to the movie in December 2015, the month of January 2016 will be devoted to viewing what promises to be a cinematic masterpiece. Watching this mega blockbuster should provide me with some clarity and direction for the coming year. Once I see the film six or seven… teen times, the rest of the year will be on Millennium Falcon cruise control.

February: On February 7th, the Super Bowl will be played at Levi's Stadium in Santa Clara. Unfortunately, the Jedi Knights will not be playing the Galactic Empire, but whichever teams end up at Super Bowl 50 this should be the biggest thing to hit the Bay Area in years and SW will definitely be taking a back seat to SB50.

I've also heard a rumor that Cupid plans to wear an Imperial Storm Trooper costume this year and instead of a bow and arrow, expect him to be wielding a light saber. Love is in the "outer space" air.

March: I totally plan on channeling my inner Yoda and trusting "the force" to guide my NCAA basketball picks this year. Last year, I was mathematically out of contention after the first day. Sadly, I was all-in with the Cal State Northridge Matadors, but that was because I didn't have Yoda weighing in on my picks . Since monitoring my March Madness bracket is pretty much an all-consuming endeavor lasting the entire month, I hope my job doesn't expect a lot out of me.

April: Last year's Star Wars Celebration 2015 took place at the Anaheim Convention Center and I missed it while touring college campuses with our oldest daughter over Spring Break. So, this year's annual Spring Break travel adventure is to attend this year's convention via a family road trip. Once there, I plan to network with my fellow Star Wars brothers and sisters in a supportive and embracing social environment. The wife and kids can go to Disneyland.

May: With any luck, Buster, Hunter, Madison, Duffy, Brandon, Panik and Brandon can follow their Jedi master, Obi-Wan Kenobi (Bruce Bochy), as he wields his force sensitive powers during this even (2016) year. I'm confident our local boys can right the Galactic starship.

June: The start of summer and a good time to get cracking on my summer reading list. There are about a million Star Wars books available to read. Just the *Jedi Apprentice* series alone has 20 volumes. *The Rising Force, The Dark Rival, The Hidden Past, The Mark of the Crown, The Defenders of the Dead, The Uncertain Path, The Captive Temple, The Day of Reckoning, The Fight for Truth, The Shattered Peace, The Deadly Hunter, The Evil Experiment, The Dan-*

gerous Rescue, The Ties That Bind, The Death of Hope, The Call to Vengeance, The Only Witness, The Threat Within, Special Edition #1: Deceptions, and *Special Edition #2: The Followers.* Once I'm done with this series, I plan to start in on *The Life and Legend of Obi-Wan Kenobi.*

July: Like every soon-to-be fifty-four-year-old, I plan to have a Star Wars-themed birthday party with all my friends where we'll all dress up like their favorite SW character. I of course will be Hans Solo. I may even invite my arch nemesis and least favorite co-worker to the party just to play the role of the evil Kylo Ren. I have seven months to teach my dog to walk on his hind legs in hopes of playing Chewbacca.

August: Summer vacation is just about over. No more stargazing at outdoor sleep outs. No more lightsaber battles with flash lights crammed inside an empty holiday wrapping paper role. No more spending days watching Star Wars marathons in a blacked down play room imagining we're battling Darth Vader for space supremacy. I didn't mean me doing this type of stuff. Why would you think it's me? It's just an example of what some kids might be doing before school starts up again.

September: Back to school. Even young Jedi Knights had to go to Rebel Alliance school before they could unleash the Rebel Fleet (kind of like their football team) on the Dark Side at the second Death Star stadium. I just hope that the current line-up of Rey, Finn and Poe Dameron can "ball" like the old guys. Don't be so quick to rush to judgement. You don't know me!

October: Halloween, hello? You get three guesses what I'll be dressed up as and   C-3PO would be wrong. If anyone guessed Jabba the Hutt you just hurt my feelings. I actually lost three pounds in 2015. I'm already building my BB-8 robot friend to accompany me to all the cool parties we'll be invited to this year.

November: Our wedding anniversary. Refer to birthday party ideas in July.

December: Santa Skywalker and Princess Leia Claus will be spreading Christmas cheer throughout the universe during the month and that's the approach I'll take. My mission will be to share holiday greetings and Ewok cheer throughout the universe or at least the Tri-Valley.

One Writer's Voice

My #1 New Year's Resolution is to watch fewer singing competitions on television. Is it cheesy to admit that I like *The Voice, American Idol* and *The Sing-Off*? Actually, only *The Voice* is still on, but I resolve to stop watching that incredibly entertaining NBC reality singing show where the winner goes on to do absolutely nothing with his/her career except to occasionally pop up on the next season of *The Voice* to promote a CD we'll never buy. The truth is, after eleven seasons, there's never been a Carrie Underwood, Kelly Clarkson, Jennifer Hudson or even a Chris Daughtry (American Idols) in the entire *Voice* bunch. That's probably a little unfair. I'm confident the past winners have sung their share of National Anthems at minor league ballparks and monster truck rallies. I bet there's been the occasional ribbon cutting at a Piggly-Wiggly grand opening. Then, of course, there's the prestigious gig of being the celebrity judge at a bowling alley karaoke competition. Sadly, I don't think I've heard so much as a single single on the radio by any of the past winners from The Voice. That said, I still like the show for a variety of reasons. For those of you keeping score, the past winners look a little something like this:

SEASON 1: JAVIER COLON.
SEASON 2: JERMAINE PAUL
SEASON 3 CASSADEE POPE
SEASON 4: DANIELLE BRADBERY
SEASON 5: TESSANNE CHIN
SEASON 6: JOSH KAUFMAN
SEASON 7: CRAIG WAYNE BOYD
SEASON 8: SAWYER FREDERICKS
SEASON 9: JORDAN SMITH
SEASON 10: ALISAN PORTER

I remember every single one of those past winners, except maybe Jermaine, Danielle and Josh, but that's because I'm into this stuff. Seeing an actual show taping is high (#4) on my bucket list and I'm not getting any younger. Just for the record, I have actually seen two alumni of *The Voice* perform live and in concert. Season 8 winner, Sawyer Fredericks, played a corporate event at Bishop Ranch and I took my daughter to see Matt McAndrew (season 7 runner-up) open for the Plain White T's last year at Slim's in San Francisco. My review? Matt had very strong vocals and was very entertaining and Sawyer was inexperienced and slightly off-key. My favorite contender of all time, you ask? That was Will Champlin. He got robbed and finished third in season 5. I don't know what he's doing today, but I hope he's got a microphone in his hand and not a speculum.

I'm actually watching the Season 11 finale as I bang out this article on my laptop. Season 11 has been a good one and I think it's safe to say that I like this season's Final Four as much as any other Final Four I've seen in the past. I'm avoiding choosing a favorite because, based on past experience, it's too emotionally draining filled with an exhausting array of the cheers and tears. I wish all the contestants good luck as I know I will never see any of them again. Fast forward to the next night, and your Season 11 winner is . . . wait for it . . . Sundance Head. There is an overwhelming abundance of applause and fanfare as the winner's family rushes the stage. Mr. Head does his best to perform his soon to be released single, available on iTunes, as confetti rains down on the stage. Despite this winning singer having a name more suited for the adult film industry, he's actually a charming and talented country troubadour. It was nice knowing you, Sundance.

Speaking of reality shows, it's hard to believe the former star of *The Apprentice* will be our next president. What? I think Adam Levine and Blake Shelton, judges on *The Voice*, should run in

2020. They could represent the Music-tarian ticket. Why not, the reality President precedent has been set. I find it hilarious that Donald Trump prepared for being leader of the free world by evaluating B-list celebrity's business abilities with the tagline, "You're Fired!" That was after he and his spawn humiliated them in the board room. I'm also amused by how upset The Donald gets at Alec Baldwin's portrayal of him on *Saturday Night Live* immediately followed by a Twitter-Tantrum. Here's some Presidential advice from a guy who was once President of the Crow Canyon Swim Team, stop watching *SNL*. When I knew someone didn't like how I was running the swim country, I avoided that person at every swim meet and social event. I never read their emails and I certainly didn't pick up my mobile phone thanks to Caller ID. I intentionally bumped more than one kid into the pool just to create a momentary distraction enabling me to escape a possible confrontation. Hopefully President Trump will be too busy not upsetting China to watch late night sketch comedy once he takes office, but I digress.

I have this reoccurring dream that I am a contestant on *The Voice*. I have this really cool Justin-Bieber-meets-Sammy-Hagar type voice and of course I get a "four-chair" turn. For those of you unfamiliar with the concept of the show, a four-chair turn is pretty much the most awesome thing that can happen during your blind audition. Anyway, I choose Miley Cyrus to be my coach, just because my daughters loved Hannah Montana growing up and I was a fan of her "Wrecking Ball" video. Creepy, I know. Sadly, I don't end up winning *The Voice* in my dream, but that's ok, because I didn't want to vanish into singing obscurity anyway. I'm already living a life in writing obscurity and a guy can only take so much obscurity. The New Year means another season of my favorite show and I can hardly wait for *The Voice* to resume. .…. If I was going to watch it, which I'm not, because I never break a New Year's resolution.

8 The Valentine's Day Advice Column

As Valentine's Day approaches, many men are filled with a certain amount of anxiety trying to find just the right token of their love and affection for their wife, girlfriend, or partner. A card is expected, as are flowers and chocolates in some cases, but what about lingerie, dinner out or jewelry? Just to clarify, those last few items are only required if you're crazy in love, dating or recently married. The question of the month is do we really need to succumb to the overwhelming holiday pressure of St. Valentine? Is it mandatory that we purchase some traditional Hallmark paraphernalia to convey our feelings of admiration and affection for the significant other in our lives, and do we expect something in return?

Allow me to assume the advice columnist role and answer all of the Valentine's Day inquiries I get every year around this time. My goal is to provide my male readers with some clarity and enlightenment in an attempt to bring you all the love and appreciation you desire. Please address your questions to Doctor Valentine's Day or just Dr. VD. No…wait, that doesn't sound quite right. Captain VD? No, I'm not a Superhero unless you consider my "love" skills to be . . . Never mind. Mr. VD? That's better.

Dear Mr. VD, I'm as romantic as the next guy, but my wife never seems to appreciate my Valentine's Day gifts. Every year, I do my best to find my wife something special, but it never fails that I somehow let her down. Is a George Foreman grill or a Paula Dean crock pot such a horrible gift? She loves to cook and I love to eat. Aren't I technically bringing us closer together? Signed, **Kitchen Casanova**.

Dear Kitchen Casanova, you're driving the right car, but just heading down the wrong road. Even Guy Fieri and Gina De Laurentiis enjoy a meal out from time to time. Pick a cool little restaurant to take her to (Baci in Danville, Salvadote Restorante in Walnut Creek or Casa Orozco in Dublin) and tell her the food won't compare to what she makes for you on a nightly basis, but you wanted to give her a night off to show your appreciation. You might want to take your dessert to go, if you know what I mean?

Dear Mr. VD, I go all out every year with the gifts. Victoria's Secret, the Shane Company and FTD Florists know me and my credit card intimately. That said, in return I usually get some lame coupon book for free hugs, a foot massage and a "day off" that I've never once tried to actually redeem. How do I get some gift appreciation this year? Signed, **Even Steven**

Dear Even Steven, I hear ya bro! You obviously take good care of your woman when it comes to the cool love-swag department. Going on the assumption that she just needs some gift ideas, I'd suggest making a list and have one of the kids pass it along to her. Golf lessons, Warriors tickets or a gift card to Buffalo Wild Wings shouldn't be expecting too much. I bet once she gets some ideas, she'll go "all in."

Dear Mr. VD, because I've always bought my two daughters cards, flowers and a little token of my fatherly love, they think Valentine's Day is like Christmas-light. Granted, Cupid is a younger, shorter, diaper wearing version of Santa, but Santa-like none the less. At what age do I remind my teenage she-devils that the little man is also armed with a nasty *Hunger Games* type crossbow and if they don't start acting more appreciative to me and my baby mama they might just get an arrow in the as...

..,backside? Signed, **Cupid Claus.**

Dear Cupid Claus, You're stuck, brother. The bond between father and daughter is precious and should never be broken even if it costs you a little scratch (aka money) on a bogus capitalistic holidays created by greedy retailers. Buy your flowers at Safeway, your cards at Party City and as for gifts, KISS – Keep it Simple Stupid. $37.50 max per kid. Gift cards or cereal are always good options. The little monsters will eventually come around and see what a great dad they have in you.

Dear Mr. VD, My gal has a smoking hot bod and I'm all about the lacy nighttime apparel, but sadly she never buys me anything sexy. Granted, I'm five-foot-six and tipping the scales at about 263 pounds, but I like to look pretty too. It hurts my feelings that she never gives me a set of silk boxer shorts or a satin robe when I've maxed out my Frederick's of Hollywood charge account on little things for her. Signed, **Sad Sack.**

Dear Sad Sack, I feel your pain. I'm not the Calvin Klein underwear model I used to be either. That said, I like to look good for my lady when we have some romantic alone time. Maybe if you drop her a hint, perhaps leave the computer logged on to the Lingerie Diva website. They have a dynamite men's page. I know this because of a little thing called research. Hopefully she'll get the message and pick you up something thongtacular this year.

Dear Mr. VD, My life partner and I have always exchanged heartfelt handwritten cards and small gifts that have some sentimental significance in our lives. We make an effort to do something together; such as see a movie or go for a hike and then in the evening we have a family dinner with the kids. Is that wrong? Should we be doing more on this romantic holiday? Signed, **Simple Life**

Dear Simple Life, You and your partner are my Valentine's Day heroes! You've got exactly the right idea of what this "holiday" should be about and signify. We don't need to load up with See's candy (although I do love See's candy) and cheesy cards to express our love. As busy as our lives are, sincerity and togetherness should mean more than a heart shaped mylar balloon, a bouquet of rose shaped chocolate-chip cookies or a mangy stuffed animal. Heart on my brothers, heart on!

Obviously, I'm not a real advice columnist. I only play one in the magazine. However, it's been reported by many sources that kids and spouses spell LOVE, T-I-M-E. Time together is the most important way to spend a holiday whose theme is love. Love who you love and let those that you love know how much you love them by being present, not giving presents. See what I did there? Take it from Mr. VD, Valentine's Day done right can leave a lasting impression the rest of the year… or at least until St. Patrick's Day. Then it's all about drinking to excess, celebrating with that deranged little leprechaun and kissing the Blarney Stone. I can't wait!

9 I'm a Yankee Doodle

> Yankee Doodle went to town
> A-riding on a pony,
> Stuck a feather in his cap
> And called it macaroni.
> Yankee Doodle keep it up,
> Yankee Doodle dandy,
> Mind the music and the step,
> And with the girls be handy.

What's a Yankee Doodle, you ask? If you have to ask you're not one! If you have to ask, you might be a communist (pre-ISIS/Jihad American hate group). I'll tell you what a Yankee Doodle is, not because I should have to, but because I have 1,200 words to fill. A Yankee Doodle is a patriot, someone proud to be an American. A Yankee Doodle can be any race, religion or ethnicity, but they must bleed red, white and blue, and damn it that's me! When you drop a Yankee Doodle on someone they instinctively think of the song. The earliest known version of the Yankee Doodle song lyrics dates back to somewhere between 1755 and 1758. It was a big hit on i-Tunes - the pre Revolutionary War playlist.

The song "Yankee Doodle Dandy" gained popularity when the Union soldiers sang it while marching during the Civil War. The confederate soldiers were probably belting out "Sweet Home Alabama." Post war, it became a unifying tune throughout the country. Although the term became a call for national unity, today's "Y Doodles" are equally proud to be from a state as great as California. Taking it one step further, we now have more regional Dandies inherently proud to be a Danvillian or an Alamoian, a San Ramonian or a Walnut Creekian. Are you picking up what I'm laying down? 2015 Yankee Doodles rocks their allegiance to country, state, city and community. They raise their flag for the good old USA, the Golden State and home region such as The Tri Valley, Blackhawk, Diablo, Rossmoor, Lamorinda, etc.

If you're ever read one of my articles in this magazine, and I'm confident at least six people have, you know I don't share my views on politics, religion, other species or extraterrestrials. Just for the record, they exist. I've seen them. Being a Yankee Doodle is more of a patriotic life choice than a club affiliation. It's a swagger we embrace because we know, for all our nation/state or town's flaws, compared to the rest of the world, there's no better place to live on planet earth than where we are today!

The list of Yankee Doodles is long and esteemed. John Wayne was a Yankee Doodle. Ronald Reagan, Amelia Earhart and Dick Clark…all Yankee Doodles. I know Walt Disney was a Yankee Doodle because I once saw Jiminy Cricket dressed up for Fourth of July in Uncle Sam attire. That little bug sure could sing and dance. Bruce Springsteen is a Doodle along with Joe Montana, Harrison Ford and my old college football coach – Jim Fairchild. I could name hundreds, maybe thousands of men and women who doodle themselves. Wait, that came out wrong.

The following is a sampling of just a few whom I considered to be Yankee Doodlers. In addition to me and my cousins Bill & Ben Seeker, the list includes Neil Armstrong, Chris Kyle, Jimmy Fallon, Madison Bumgarner & Buster Posey, Clint Eastwood, Sandra Bullock, Hulk Hogan, Toby Keith, Jon Stewart, Charlie Brown & Snoopy, The entire Curry family (Steph, Ayesha, Del, hot Sonya and adorable little Riley), Bob Costas, John Grisham, Chris Rock, Kid Rock, Duane "The Rock" Johnson, Danica Patrick, Rudolf Giuliani, Captain America, Captain Crunch, Howard Stern, Tom Brokaw and Beyonce.

A Yankee Doodle is a Patriotic person. **Fiona D., age 11**

A Yankee Doodle is a rag in the shape of a swirl hat. **Brandon C., age 6 ½**

A Yankee Doodle is some kind of noodle food. **Jessica C., age 8**

A Yankee Doodle is a cartoon character macaroni guy. **Hannah O., age 10**

A Yankee Doodle is a lady wearing a hat with feathers riding a horse down a dirt road. **Taylor O., age 8**

A Yankee Doodle is a person who traded stuff with other people and became rich. **Jake A., age 10**

A Yankee Doodle is a cowboy who invents stuff. **Trevor R., age 9**

A Yankee Doodle is someone who can't do what they're trying to do. **Harper C., age almost 5.**

A Yankee Doodle is a yellow pony who eats macaroni. **Megan L., age 4 1/2**

A Yankee Doodle is an old time baseball player with the New York Yankees. **Brady L., age 7 ½.**

A Yankee Doodle is a noodle dinner with sauce that kids like to eat. **Reese M., age 6**

A Yankee Doodle is a song you sing on the Fourth of July.
Regan D., age 7

Some politicians are Doodles, but not all of them. Some politicians are just plain tools. I think it's safe to say that Olympic athletes are Yankee Doodles along with anyone in the military. Just for the record, we owe anyone in the military and our military veterans (along with their families) our full YD respect and admiration. HOO RA!

Back in the 1940s, or was it the 1840s?....doesn't matter, James "Jimmy" Cagney stared in an American biographical musical movie about the life of George M. Cohen called *Yankee Doodle Dandy*. I don't know if Cagney was a Yankee Doodle in real life, because he's dead, but my wife's aunt Peggy says Cagney was "The cat's pajamas." That could be old people speak for Yankee Doodle? I don't really speak old, people. I speak mid-life crisis. Unless I'm mistaken, it was Cagney who had the famous line, "You dirty rat!" That's kind of Doodle and gangster.

Lately, I've been binge-watching *House of Cards* and *The West Wing* on Netflix to amp up my Yankee Doodle political knowledge. I also recently caught a Netflix showing of the movie *Independence Day*. That's a fun way to totally geek-out your Americana patriotism. My Yankee Doodle pride will be on full display this Fourth of July and every day after that from here to eternity, because that's how I roll. Doodle on my brothers and sisters. Doodle on!

10 Preserving the "Magic Words" this year

Growing up, the words "please" and "thank you" were the "magic words." If you wanted something you said "please" and if you got something, you said "thank you." To six-year-old me, that made perfect sense. Hell, to Fifty-six-year-old me, it's still makes perfect sense. These are common courtesy, common decency, common sense, words that are the foundation of life lessons. I'm just troubled that these words, not to mention a boat load of other words, phrases, and expressions, are not being instilled in our children any longer. I beat those words, and others, into my daughters' heads growing up and when I say "beat" it into them, I hope everyone knows I meant that in a metaphorical way. We practiced saying please and thank you the same way we practiced breathing. Has it become too much to say please and thank You, let alone excuse me or ex-squeeze me?

The word "please" is quite pleasing to the ear. "Please" is a gracious way of requesting someone's participation. Please pass me the salt, please pick up your toys, please take a seat, please make your bed, please don't torment your sister, please drop my clothes off at the dry cleaner, please sir may I have some more, "Please Please Me" (a Beatles song) or please don't eat the daisies. Please accept this article as the best I could do given how far past the deadline I am this month. Please is an enchanting word.

The words "thank" and "you," standing alone, are just two little words, but together they show appreciation, thoughtfulness and gratitude. Thank you for your business, thank you for waiting, thank you for seeing me, thank you for coming, thank you for the gift, thank you for the donation, thank you for the help, thank you for remembering, thank you for calling, thank you for the great service, thank you sir may I have another or thank you for writing such a well thought-out and slightly humorous article? Thank you is also an endearing word.

Just for the record, "excuse me" is a polite expression; however, "ex-squeeze me" is just fun to say as long as it's not taken in a sexually harassing kind of way. If I've offended anyone, please excuse my oafish insensitivity and accept my heartfelt apology. Thank you.

When you think about the obvious times a please or thank you might be appropriate, my best advice is to start at home. Appreciate your partner for everything he, she or they do around the house. We can all fall into a rut or routine where we have our chores and they have theirs, but it never hurts to drop a please or thank you every once in awhile. It might cause someone to fall off their chair or question their hearing if they haven't heard those words in months or maybe years. The reaction might be worth the effort alone. "Honey, thank you for washing and folding my socks and t-shirts. You really get those stains out," or, "Sugar, would you please let me know if my flatulence bothers you tonight? I really shouldn't have had the bean casserole." Once you've started to make progress at home, initiate the same game plan at work.

Has a magazine column writer ever received a Yelp review? Yikes, that might be asking for trouble. I think Yelp is a worthwhile website/app, but it's not just for complaining. I probably post seven or eight positive Yelp reviews to every one or two negative. I love recognizing good service and Yelp is just one more way of saying thank you to an employee or company for exceptional service. Too many Yelp trolls love blasting out negative reviews just for the exposure or attention. Let's all make a pledge to post at least one Yelp review that's positive/appreciative. Me first: I would like to thank Belinda in Macy's accounting department for her excellent customer service in helping me resolve an overcharge for delivery. Belinda was professional, responsive, helpful, and a real problem solver. I wish more call center employees were like Miss Belinda at Macy's, but please take the time to point out when someone does so that it might encourage others to train, implement and practice.

It goes without saying that military personnel, first responders (law enforcement, firemen and paramedics) and teachers should always be thanked. They are the backbone of our society and without these brave souls on the front lines our country could fall into a state of bedlam, chaos or civil unrest. At the same time, on a completely different level, please recognize the unsung heroes that don't get the recognition they deserve. Not just veterans, but public transportation (BART, bus and ferry) drivers, mail carriers, hospice workers and some politicians, and also volunteers at every level. Food banks, Meals on Wheels, charity fun runs and youth sports programs are indebted to their volunteer work force.

As a former soccer, softball, baseball, football coach and swim team president, your kid's leagues and teams wouldn't exist without a dedicated group of parents who give countless hours to these programs. That's not to say there aren't occasional issues or problems, but suffice it to say, it's usually 20% of the parents doing 80% of the work to keep the sport operating. I've heard a lot of complaints in my day that never started with a "please" or ended with a "thank you." It's easy to be negative without any constructive ideas or personal commitment to resolve the problems. In my firsthand experience, organizations such as the San Ramon Valley Girls Athletic League ("SRVGAL softball"), Mustang Soccer and the San Ramon Valley Thunderbirds football and cheer programs are staffed by a lot of wonderfully dedicated volunteer parents that are involved for all the right reasons and those individuals deserve an occasional please and thank you.

I've been on my soapbox for about two hours now trying to

craft a positive and yet poignant first article of the new year. How and I doing? I'm far from the ideal role model and yet, I do try to practice what I preach. Please and thank you were once the norm, the basics every child was taught by parents who saw the value in manners and behavior. Please don't let these magic words die out with so many other life lessons that have fallen by the wayside. It's too easy to blame social media or the millennial generation. Let's all take responsibility to please preserve the magic words in the new year. Thank you.

11 An Astrological New Year

It's not like I plan my day around my horoscope, at least not my entire day, but I do like to check in to see what the stars have in store for me. I think we can all admit that we will check our scope from time to time while reading the newspaper. For those of you unfamiliar with a newspaper it is a black and white print periodical delivered to your home or purchased at the local smoke shop or train station. Personally, I am always encouraged when there's a positive message about my finances, health, career or relationships. Sadly, one recent morning, over a bowl of oatmeal, my wife was less than enthusiastic when I informed her that today was the day I would find my soulmate. What a buzzkill.

By definition, a horoscope is an astrological chart or diagram representing the positions of the sun, moon, planets, astrological aspects and sensitive angles at the time of an event, such as the moment of a person's birth. It is used to forecast a person's future, typically including a delineation of character and circumstances, based on the relative positions of the stars and planets on any given day. A brief daily forecast is something a large segment of the population follows on a semi-regular basis, me included.

I have always found it uncanny the way a horoscope can identify a person's personality with a high degree of accuracy. I am so the Leo personality as described below.

The Leo Personality
Bold, intelligent, warm, and courageous, fire sign Leo is a natural leader of the Zodiac, ready to blaze a trail, vanquish injustice, and make a name for themselves along the way. Blessed with high self-esteem, Lions know that they possess enviable

traits—and they're proud of them. They don't believe in false modesty and will be the first to praise themselves for a job well done. But Leo isn't self-aggrandizing or unwilling to roll up those sleeves and do the work: this sign knows that in order to be respected and admired, he or she needs to put in the effort worthy of a leader.

But it's not all hard work for Lions. Intense and energetic, Leos thrive on social interactions and have no problem making friends—although pinning them down to spend time with you is another story. Leos put themselves first, and will turn down a plan that doesn't fit with their agenda or idea of fun. This trait has gained them an unfair reputation for arrogance. But on the flip side, when a Lion chooses to spend time with you, it's genuinely because he or she wants to.

Given my bold and intelligent personality, allow me to impress you with my uniquely unqualified and misinformed attempt to predict what the year holds for each of the fourteen or fifteen Zodiac signs. What, only twelve astrological signs? What about the Houston Astros, Foo Fighters and White Walkers? World Series Champs, rock band and Game of Thrones? Whatever. Here goes nothing?

Your 2018 Horoscopes

Aries – The first sign of the Zodiac, an Aries is both passionate and independent not to mention extremely competitive. I see a year filled with hot love making, but also lots of intense solitaire games on your phone. Symbol – The ram.

Aquarius – The Zodiac's deep thinker. Aquarians are a bit bipolar in that they can be both shy and quiet and energetic and boisterous. I like that you're likely to have months of comatose down time and months of "call the cops" party time. Symbol – the water bearer.

Taurus – The anchor of the Zodiac. A Taurus is smart, ambitious and trustworthy. The stars tell me you will make wise decisions that benefit your career because co-workers know you won't throw them under the bus despite your desire to succeed. Symbol – the bull.

Virgo – The sophisticated one. Virgos get the job done without complaining. They are big picture thinkers and very good at planning out their lives. Knowing that they are amazing friends and don't like to disappoint anyone, this year will be devoted to hosting gatherings and events with people you love. I'm free. Symbol – the virgin.

Capricorn – The Zodiac considers this the most serious-minded of the signs. Capricorn's pride themselves on their professionalism and traditional values. Both conventional and independent, this could be a big year in your job or career. Don't be afraid to quit, but give at least two week's notice. Symbol – the goat.

Libra – A sign of balance within the Zodiac. Libras are peace loving and judicial. They also abhor being alone. With their winning personalities and cooperative style, this could be the year your find true love. Maybe don't mention that to your spouse. Symbol – the scales.

Pisces – The understanding Zodiac sign. Pisces are generally compassionate, gentle and affectionate. Your Facebook and LinkedIn networks will explode with likes and friend requests given your likability and ability to interact with a wide variety of personalities. Stay away from prison pen pals. Symbol – the fish.

Gemini – The chameleon of the Zodiac. Geminis are excellent communicators and adept at blending into different groups. Energetic and quick-witted, you are likely to create some form of art that makes a statement this year. If it happens to be in the written form, think Alive Book Publishing. Symbol – the twins.

Cancer - The sentimental Zodiacer. Emotions run high for

Cancers and nothing is more important than family and home. Despite a horribly unfortunate Zodiac name, your sympathetic and empathetic nature means your year will be filled with wonderful family fued-less type gatherings. Sorry. Symbol – the crab.

Leo – See the description above. The natural leader of the Zodiac. A Leo will create a game-changing community service app, rescue someone that needs a lifeline and host the hottest party of the year. Text me if you want to be on the guest list. Symbol – the lion.

Scorpio – The Zodiac's intense one. Scorpios are always caring and aware of others' feelings. They often ask probing and penetrating questions. If the moon continues to hang in the sky, I sense that you will help build and mend relationships in 2018. Start with your sister, I'm just saying. Symbol – the scorpion.

Sagittarius – The energetic one. A Sagittarius is so extroverted and broad-minded that they are always open to new experiences. Knowing that it is impossible to keep a Sag down and that change is essential to this sign's life, I see a career change for you. Have you considered ventriloquism or zoology? Symbol – the archer.

Who could do this every day? I'm exhausted. Undoubtedly you will find elements of truth and ridiculousness in your Zodiac sign above, but you try writing a game-changing New Year's article that isn't redundant or mundane. At least I'm getting some use out of my new thesaurus. I wish I could think of another word for horoscope, Zodiac or thesaurus. If you don't think my predictions accurately identify how you look, think or feel then I encourage you to live out your own aspirations and goals for the year. It's a blank slate, color it however you feel.

12 Halloweek
My Spooktacular Holiday Idea

Halloween is about so much more than just one night of dress up and trick-or-treating. This traditional fall holiday is about costumes and candy, decorations and scary movies, parties and pageantry. It's so much fun to see this haunting holiday through the eyes of a child, or you can even choose to be a kid again by participating in the festivities. What a load of PC gibberish that was. Who do I think I am, some octogenarian *60 Minutes* reporter like Mike Wallace or Morley Schaffer? Tonight on *60 Minutes* we'll investigate why Linus spends every Halloween in a deserted pumpkin patch in Peanutsville awaiting the arrival of a Santa-like gourd character known only as The Great Pumpkin. This mythical being is likely the marketing tool of some nameless diabetes drug company sent to specific suburban markets with the sole intention of getting kids hooked on sugar treats for a lifelong adult dependency on Metformin.

Humor aside, assuming any of that first paragraph was remotely humorous, I'm part of a silent minority that believes Halloween should actually be a national holiday celebrated for an entire week. At this very moment, there's an independent grassroots movement to convert one day/night into 7 days and 6 nights of ghoulish fun every year and call it Halloweek. As it is, Americans spend over $8 billion annually on candy, decorations, costumes, cards and dental related bills. Actually, it's $8,000,003,562.12 if you include my neighbor's house, but shouldn't our money stretch a little further?

Halloweek would start with every citizen of our fine country being required to dress up for all seven days. If you're living in the US of A, regardless of age, race, religion or political party you'd be required to wear a costume each and every day. While I haven't put a lot of thought into it yet, there's a good chance I would be a cowboy on Sunday, followed by a robot, a caveman, a pirate, a fireman, a lumberjack and maybe a vampire. That would be my dress-up week as I selected costumes that I thought would somewhat compatible with my primary occupation. I'm not looking to scare or disgust my clients, but simply to get into the theme of the holiday. I guarantee you no one would dress up as a commercial real estate agent or humor lifestyle columnist. That would be too boring. I know because I live it 24/7 and while at times it can be a little sad and depressing, glamorous it isn't.

Watching scary movies should also be part of the Halloweek celebration. There is scientific proof that scary movies are good for the heart, digestion and circulatory system. Cinematic masterpieces such as *Friday the 13th, The Ring, The Shining, The Exorcist, Psycho, Carrie*, and of course all seven of the *Halloween* franchise movies starring Jamie Lee Curtis would be required viewing. I'll even accept old black & white classics such as *Dracula* staring Bela Lugosi, *The Mummy* featuring Vincent Price or *The Fly* (the original, not the remake). Just for the record, *Ghostbusters, Rocky Horror Picture Show, Young Frankenstein*, Michael Jackson's "Thriller" video and the live action Scooby-Doo do not qualify as a scary movies. Watching Freddie Prinze Jr. as Fred and Sarah Michelle Gellar as Daphne run around town in lame '70s outfits with a CGI/animated Great Dane is just wasting two hours on a Saturday I'll never get back. A scary movie needs to elicit bowel-churning anxiety while watching the action through the cracks in your finger mask with the family room lights turned out – a dark room adds to the viewing experience.

Handing out candy to trick-or-treaters is about as All-American as the UFC Fight Night, Chick-fil-A and Honda cars. During my week-long Halloweek master plan, T-o-Ting would however be limited to just two days for two specific reasons. #1. Two (2) days is necessary in case a trick-or-treater gets sick or has a scouts/band/sports/school/church conflict on one of the days and (B) Trick or Treating for any more than two days would just be easy pickings for the dentists in our community.

Now, it's also about time we set a minimum standard for giveaway candy. Back in my day, aka the good old days, mini candy bars (Milky Way, Three Musketeers, Snickers, Mounds, Almond Joy, Kit Kat, Baby Ruth and $100,000 bars) were about twice the size of what they are today. What is this world coming to, when candy bar companies determine that mini isn't mini enough so over time they slowly make these delicious morsels mini-er? Being a candy aficionado myself, I do enjoy me some Skittles, Jolly Ranchers, Starbursts and Twizzlers. Hold on for one minute. I'm not saying Twizzlers are as satisfying as Red Vines and black licorice, but I've grown to appreciate "the Twiz," especially since The American Licorice Company doesn't produce a Trick-or-Treat portion size that I'm aware of. Where we stray into unacceptable territory, is when people try and pass out raisins, an assortment of nuts or popcorn balls. That's just not right! In fact, that's just someone asking for their pumpkin to be kicked in or an egg rainstorm to befall their driveway.

Pumpkins will continue to be another favorite element of Halloweek, but not just carving Jack-O-Lanterns. I'm not opposed to a Hannibal Lecter-type face skinning and brain-goop dissection of a big ripe pumpkin, but there's just so many more delicious baking options to this delectable vegetable including pumpkin pie, spice bread, cookies, Bundt cakes and even pumpkin based CBD oils and incense. My pink eye and gout cleared right up when I recently smoked a bowl of pumpkin seeds.

When it comes to Halloweek decorations, the mo the better. Drape those orange and purple lights across your house like it's that December holiday that encourages festive outdoor light displays. Install as many blow-ups, pop-ups and rise-from-the-dead fake graveyards as your front yard can support or your

HOA will allow. I'm all about trying to create an audio and visual cemetery scene that will induce every elementary schooler to mess their pants if they pass by it at night. I'm not saying that happened to me in October of 1973, but my sister does claim to have some type of proof she's willing to release if I ever decide to run for public office.

It's a little known fact that many other countries have already transitioned to the Halloweek concept. My good friend, Cliff Clavin, informed me that several nations in Eastern Europe and the Kurdistan region, such as Latvia, Moldova, Albania, Azerbaijan or was it Kazakhstan (?), Disneyland and Transylvania have all embraced a weeklong celebration leading up to the Day of the Dead. Transylvania was an easy one. The Magical Kingdom actually celebrates for an entire two months and they wear costumes year round. Truthfully, most countries don't celebrate Halloween. Why not, you ask? My deadline is nearing and I don't have time to Wiki research that question, but suffice it to say, we should consider ourselves lucky to enjoy such a frivolous and decadent one day celebration consisting of candy and dress up hedonism. Halloweek may never get off the ground, but I hope everyone enjoys a spooktacular Halloween.

13 If I Lived at the North Pole

Bless Santa's heart for choosing such an obscure location for his world headquarters, but he's got to have a few neighbors who don't work for him at the North Pole. There's probably a Farmers Insurance agent, a cop and fireman, maybe even a CVS store manager. If somehow I ended up living in the neighborhood, I might also be a bit concerned about my Wi-Fi connectivity, my Dish satellite reception, my access to a Peet's Coffee and how far a sleigh ride is it to the nearest 24 Hour Fitness?

If I lived at the North Pole, I would get a job at Santa's factory. **Tyler H., Age 6**

If I lived at the North Pole, I would run away. **Colton M., Age 8**

Similar to the civic courting Amazon has recently received (238 proposals) for their second headquarters site, the Economically Development Department at the North Pole City Hall must have put together one heck of an impressive economic incentive package when swaying Santa from his previous location. There must also have been perks galore from the North Pole Chamber of Commerce and the North Pole Owner's Association, because why else would you choose such a challenging place to set up shop....a work shop? Employee retention could be one reason, perhaps the only reason. I don't mean to be politically incorrect, but where else does a large population of elves reside? In the big picture, it does make sense to locate close to your employee base and unless I'm mistaken, I don't think there's a big magical elf population in Texas, Nevada or Michigan just to name a few of the other potential suitors for Santa's Apple-like campus.

If I lived at the North Pole, I would visit Santa every day and I would give him presents to give to the kids. **Justin L., Age 6**

If I lived at the North Pole, I would find Santa and build ice sculptures. **Lucus T., Age 7**

If I lived the North Pole, I would go see Santa and help him make presents. **Caden R., Age 9**

If I lived at the North Pole, I would help the elves make toys and then help deliver them and then I would do it again the next year and the next year and the next year. **Ava A., Age 5**

If I lived at the North Pole, I would find Santa's castle and ask him to make me an elf. **Maddox G., Age 7**

I've been enjoying some pleasant late fall weather the last few weeks of November. Chilly mornings, comfortable afternoons and cool evenings are indicative of this time of year. Some (me) say autumn is the nicest time of year to visit the greater Bay Area. Rumor has it that Santa and Mrs. Claus were seen in Walnut Creek around Thanksgiving. Granted, we don't get to experience the delightful seasonal weather changes of places such as the Rocky Mountains, the Pacific Northwest, or the East Coast, but we get more variety than the North Pole. Can you imagine spending 365 days a year living at the North Pole? Well, 350 days, given two weeks for vacation and one very busy workday of travel. I think the term "white-out" was conceived in the North Pole when a local mommy went to pick up the kids from school and couldn't find the school because it was covered in snow.

The North Pole is located in the middle of the Arctic

Ocean amid waters that are almost permanently covered with constantly shifting sea ice. Winter temperatures at the North Pole can range from about −50 to −13 °C (−58 to 9 °F), averaging around −31 °C (−24 °F)-and summer temperatures (June, July, and August) average around the freezing point (0 °C (32 °F). I could be wrong, although I rarely am, but I doubt there's a lot of variation in the temperature during the spring or fall.

If I lived at the North Pole, I would freeze to death, **Grayson G., Age 9**

If I lived at the North Pole, I would build a fire every day. **Pierce B., Age 6**

It's said that home is where the heart is, but wouldn't my heart be mighty cold at such a desolate snow-centric location? Housing might be inexpensive; however, can you imaging what my PG&E bill would run every month? I doubt solar is an option. It must be murder (6-9 month wait) to get an appointment with a furnace and insulation contractor.

If I lived at the North Pole, I would make an igloo house. **Caleb S., Age 8**

If I lived at the North Pole, I would make friends with the animals and the Elves, **Zoe O., Age 7**

On the positive side, my sock and sweater collection would undoubtedly be impressive. I like socks, but sweaters make me look a little bulky. By bulky, I mean that visually I appear to weigh about 350 lbs. in a nice cardigan. If I grew a white beard and wore a red sweater, the big man might have a doppelgänger roaming the streets of the Pole.

If I'm getting technical, and I do like to get technical, the North Pole, also known as the Geographic North Pole or Terrestrial North Pole, is defined as the point in the Northern Hemisphere where the Earth's axis of rotation meets its surface. The South Pole on the other hand, lies on the opposite side of the Earth from the North Pole. Now I don't know if the North Pole and South Pole relationship is quiet as contentious as North and South Korea or North and South Dakota, but for the purpose of this article I'm going to assume it's all cool between the two Poles. See what I did there? "All cool," get it? That said, there's got to be a little Santa envy coming from the south. There's no real government faction that rules the South Pole, largely because there's no indigenous peoples and no one lives there permanently, but somewhere there's a lonely scientist in a remote South Pole arctic research station pissed off because he can't hang with Santa and the elves at the local sports bar like his northern counter-part.

Should we one day look to downsize and relocate, the North Pole will not likely be one of our potential senior community destinations, I really like Bend, Oregon, personally; however, I will keep an open mind. It will ultimately depend on where our kids end up settling and if that turns out to be the North Pole, then anything is possible. Have a happy holiday season.

14 Thanksgiving Carols

Every Thanksgiving, I like to gather my loved ones around the antique Costco electronic keyboard to sing a few of the endearing Thanksgiving Day songs we sang as kids. You all undoubtedly remember those cheery carols that bring the holiday to life, feuding families together and providing a much-needed break in the nonstop food consumption trying to avoid the dreaded food coma.

Unless you were raised in England and still harbor angry feelings toward the Pilgrims for moving away from home to a cool new land, you undoubtedly love all things Thanksgiving. I sure do. Should you be unfamiliar with the story, let me remind you that in 1621 the Plymouth colonists and Wampanoag Indians shared an autumn harvest feast that is acknowledged today as one of the first Thanksgiving celebrations in the colonies. For more than two centuries, days of thanksgiving have been celebrated throughout these United States. I should have been a history teacher.

Unless I'm mistaken, Thanksgiving carols were originated the evening of that first Thanksgiving. Granted, there was a slight language barrier, but both the Plymouth colonists and the Wampanoag Indians soon found common ground as they sat around the fire pit harmonizing and gorging on pumpkin pie with Cool Whip. I hope these traditional songs bring you the same joy that others get when I break into song and sing as loud as I can at the office, the grocery store or in the gym.

Tommy the Turkey (sang to "Frosty the Snowman")

Tommy the Turkey, was a hearty healthy treat
From a cornfed ranch he loved to dance

On two drumsticks of dark meat

Tommy the Turkey, was a Butterball they say
If you liked a thigh or breast, you could never rest
Fighting all the hungry guests that day

There must have been some gravy on the stove yet to be found
For when Uncle Bob reached for the bowl
He began to dance around

Tommy the Turkey
Was as alive as he could be
Until the butcher came and he was slain
to make a family's feast complete.

In addition to eating, eating and more eating on Thanksgiving Day, my family enjoys the occasional break to digest, rest and reset. This is when we typically watch a little football on the tiny eighty-inch flatscreen. I bet you didn't know that the University of Detroit stadium hosted the first broadcasted Thanksgiving Day football game in 1934, pitting the Detroit Lions against the Chicago Bears and sparking a new holiday tradition. Currently, three NFL games are played every Thanksgiving. The first two are hosted by the Detroit Lions and the Dallas Cowboys; a third game, with no fixed opponents, has been played annually since 2006. I should have been an NFL history teacher. The next little ditty goes back almost as far back as that first game in 1934.

Football Games (Sung to "Jingle Bells")

Rushing through the house
For the first game of the day

Over the couch I go
snacking all the way
Smells from ovens waft
making bellies growl
it's so much fun to cheer my team
while chugging spirits down

Football games, football games
Football games today
Oh what fun it is to watch
The Lions fade away
Football games, football games
Football games today
Oh what fun it is to watch
The Cowboys lay an egg

Once the traditional day of fun, family, football, and foul consumption is completed and the festivities are over, it's time to get back to a regular dietary routine for a week or two until the Christmas and Hanukah parties begin. This delightful sing-along really sets the tone for the weeks leading up to the next caloric catastrophe.

Jenny Craig is coming to Town (sung to "Santa Claus is Coming to Town")

You ate helpings galore
You reached for the pie
Buttered your bread
You thought you might die
Jenny Craig is coming to town

You devoured the bird
The stuffing was nice
She's gonna find out who ate gravy with rice
Jenny Craig is coming to town

She sees you when you are snacking
She knows when you eat cake
She knows when you sneak late at night
So be careful what you bake

You better work out
You better not lie
You better not booze
I'm telling you why
Jenny Craig is coming to town

There are obviously countless more traditional holiday songs that I could share with you, but I have an eight hundred-word limit. Suffice it to say, any one of the following tunes could be your family favorite.

Do You Eat What I Eat? (sung to "Do You Hear What I Hear?")
O Come, All Ye Hungry (sung to "O Come, All Ye Faithful")
Joy to the Bathroom (sung to "Joy to the World")
Oh Little Mall of Pleasanton (sung to "Little Town of Bethlehem")
What Movie is on? (sung to "What Child Is This?")

Regardless what songs you and your family or friends sing this Thanksgiving season, remember it's about the spirit of the holiday and sharing memories with loved ones because no one ever wrote a holiday song about Black Friday.

IV

Music and Musicians

I love music, but I am not a musician. "Don't be late for band practice" is a phrase I've never heard—nor will I ever. My lack of talent only makes me more envious and respectful of those who possess those God-given genes. Since I can't write (or play) music, I enjoy writing about musicians. I possess the God-given profile writing gene that can give a musician, or their band, free exposure. Also, much like Lex Luther, I get to pull back the cape, in a non-sexual way, to learn about how they acquired and honed their super powers.

Attending concerts has always been my vice. Well, one of my many vices. I have always enjoyed seeing and hearing music live in small clubs or large arenas and amphitheaters. I have seen over a hundred shows and look forward to many more to come. When I was a kid, I was happy just to be at the venue and I would gladly sit anywhere. Now that I'm a semi-successful writer and businessman going through a mid-life crisis, I will pay more money to sit in good seats. Candidly, I wouldn't enjoy the experience if I was seated in the nosebleeds.

1

Paul Jefferson
A Nashville Singer/Songwriter with Bay Area Roots

Nashville singer-songwriter Paul Jefferson will be headlining Discovery Counseling Center's fifth annual fall fundraiser, An Evening of Laughter and Music. Paul is an accomplished country artist, as a solo performer, a duo and as part of a popular band. However, it's Paul's songwriting talent that has kept him in high demand in and around Nashville for the past twenty years. Paul has written songs with the likes of Keith Urban, Little Texas, Jon Bon Jovi, Timothy B. Schmitt (Eagles), Jane Wiedlin and Charlotte Caffey (Go-Go's), and Buddy Jewel, to name just a few. He co-wrote Aaron Tippin's number one song, "That's As Close As I'll Get To Loving You." Not bad for a kid from Northern California.

I first met Paul Jefferson Jaqua in the spring of 1989 at a little coffee shop in Mountain View. A mutual friend, Steve Silver, convinced me to check out this aspiring country artist whose brother was the starting quarterback on our community college football team. County music was beginning a surge in popularity with the emergence of such popular acts as Garth Brooks, The Judds, Travis Tritt, Brooks & Dunn and the band Restless Heart along with the more established artists which included George Strait, Alan Jackson, Alabama and Reba McIntire. I'll admit my expectations were relatively low, knowing that Paul had grown up in Woodside, CA playing tennis and learning to fly while earning a Biomedical degree at Cal. However, the minute he hit the stage, I could tell by his old school country sound and appeal that audiences would gravitate toward such an authentic performer. Over the next couple of years, I became Paul's booking agent, merchandise manager, publicist, roadie, bodyguard and confidant. It wasn't until the unexpected death of our good friend Steve that Paul would leave the comfort of the Bay Area to pursue his dreams in Nashville. "When Steve died, I knew I couldn't live with myself if I didn't push myself and give Nashville a chance," Paul recalls with a heavy heart.

Before leaving for Nashville, Paul played a lot of small clubs and cafes around the South Bay. "Playing those blood buckets was tough. More than a few were barely keeping the doors open trying to capitalize on the popularity of country music," says Paul. "What made it bearable was playing with a lot of really good people and talented musicians." A highlight during those early times was when he was cast as Hank Williams in the San Jose Stage Company's production of *Lost Highway*. Paul's connection to the music of Hank Williams would live on for the next twenty-five years.

Originally signed as a songwriter by a Los Angeles based publishing house in 1993, Paul was flown to Nashville to perform a collection of original songs at the legendary Bluebird Cafe. While in Nashville, he was recording demos and performing new material with a session vocalist named Steve McClintock, a slightly older music veteran. The pair was quickly offered a record deal, as a duo, *Jefferson McClintock*. Paul had fewer reservations about dropping his given last name, Jaqua, than he did becoming part of a duo, so he passed on the offer. Oddly, Paul has certain regrets about both of those decisions to this day.

Paul Jefferson signed a management contract with legendary music manager Miles Copeland (no relation) who had managed The Police, REM, The Go-Go's and The English Beat. "Miles was new to Nashville and looking for country artists. He also signed a young Keith Urban," Paul recalls. Shortly thereafter, Paul released his first CD with Almo Records and his first single, *Check Please*, hit number 40 on the country music charts. Sadly, Paul was going through some personal and professional struggles just as his video for *Check Please* made its debut on CMT (Country Music Television), which didn't allow him to truly enjoy a lot of his early success. He parted ways with both his management team and Almo, and eventually went on to record and self-release his follow-up album; *Greatest Hits Volume III* which he says is a record he is extremely proud of due to the strength of the songs. This trying period did open the door to writing sessions with Sonny Lemaire of the band Exile, John Scott Sherrill (Paul's all-time favorite songwriter) and Porter Howell of the band, Little Texas. His work with Porter eventually led to the foundation of their group, Hilljack.

Paul likes to say he and Porter just clicked when it came to writing and performing. Hilljack released an independent record, but had a major league management and booking team. This allowed the band to tour the U.S. and Europe opening for some of country music's biggest names including; Dwight Yokum, John Berry and Wynonna Judd. Unfortunately, after little more than a year, and just as the band's popularity and success was starting to take off, Little Texas reunited and Porter left Hilljack to rejoin his original band. Try as he might to replace his good friend, the chemistry was never the same with other guitarists and the band eventually broke up.

Paul met the immensely talented and very successful Canadian country artist, Lisa Brokup, in 2008. She and Paul were married twenty-four months later and the couple has a daughter, Ivy, who just turned 7 years old. When asked if Ivy can sing, Paul gave the response, "She's very loud, but she prefers to dance." Lisa and Paul regularly write together and perform regionally and around Nashville as a duo, *The Jeffersons.* Their debut album, *The Jefferson's Vol. 1*, was released in June of 2011 by Royalty Records to very strong reviews. Today, Lisa is enjoying success performing in a critically acclaimed Patsy Cline tribute and the couple takes turns touring so that one of them is always home with their daughter.

Throughout the course of our interview, I juggled the role of journalist with friend and fan. When I asked Paul how he felt about the success of the ABC series *Nashville*, he indicated that it's brought a lot of new fans to country music and packs the venues around town, but he admitted that it feels the storylines hit just a little too close to home. "I feel, in a way, like the show is imitating my life." When I asked if he has a favorite song that he's written or one that he's most proud of, "You're Not My God" was his immediate response. The song was written with and recorded by Keith Urban. Paul candidly revealed that the song is about addiction. "Keith and I are both in recovery and it's a song about conquering your demons. It's inspired a lot of people, and that's something that really means a lot to me." Knowing that Paul has played the Grand Ole Opry twice (solo and with Hilljack), I asked him if that was the pinnacle of his career. While he acknowledged that playing there was a wonderful experience, he recalled a tour opening for Trisha Yearwood in Europe. "Playing the Civic Center Opera House in Birmingham, England was the greatest performing experience of my life. It was a magnificent theater with absolutely perfect sound," Paul recalls.

I also inquired about the cross-over pop appeal of such country artists as Taylor Swift, Florida Georgia Line, Lady Antebellum and The Zack Brown Band. Paul never expressed any animosity or jealousy, but he did say the music market goes through cycles. "A lot of the new songs are catchy and they appeal to the younger buyers, but it's gotten away from the music came here to make. Music goes through cycles and it will eventually come back to pure country."

When it comes to the pure country sound, it doesn't get any more pure than the music of Hank Williams. Over the years, Paul has often talked about how much he loved performing as Hank in the *Lost Highway* production in the early 90s. It's with this in mind, along with his wife Lisa's success with the Patsy

Cline project, that Paul has begun working on a Hank tribute. "This isn't a play where I have to portray Hank in his 20s, it's just me doing Hank songs, and a few of my own that were inspired by Hank." The Hank project has already received a lot of advance buzz, and Paul hopes to launch a tour early next year. Until then, he is always in demand to collaborate with his peers and for a guy with Bay Area roots that's pretty flattering and impressive.

2 David Victor
Rock Stars & Stripes

Walnut Creek native and Northgate High School alumnus, David Victor, is a bona-fide rock star as a former member of the legendary rock band Boston. Yes, *that* Boston. The "More Than a Feeling," "Don't Look Back," "Peace of Mind," and "Amanda" Boston who dominated the AM/FM air waves from the late 1970s to the mid-1990s and are still a staple on classic rock radio playlists. Today, David is still rocking out, but also giving back through rock music.

David moved to L.A. to pursue a career in music after graduating from Cal State East Bay with a degree in Computer Science. After modest success with the band Velocity, David played with the Boston tribute band Smokin', where he was discovered through a YouTube video by Boston's founding member, Tom Scholz. David spent five years with the band and was featured as the lead vocalist on their #1 classic-rock charting single "Heaven on Earth" from their 2014 album *Life, Love & Hope*. I caught up with him recently at Side Board in Danville to talk about his Boston experience, and to hear more about his current project, Rock Stars & Stripes.

What was it like playing with Boston? Did you do a big tour of large venues?

I joined Boston in late 2009, and we did a couple of North American tours with the band in 2012 and 2014. We rehearsed in north Boston for several weeks before I did my first show in Hollywood, Florida in 2012. Rehearsing with the whole band was a trip. The lineup was not settled. I thought they were going to ship me out the first day! But I stuck around. One of my vivid memories was working with Tom Scholz who wrote "Peace of Mind," my favorite Boston song ever. Of course,

I learned way more than I ever could possibly have given back, most importantly exactly how the guitar parts went from the guy who wrote them!

The two tours I did were amazing, but the Boston Strong show was especially moving, because some of the survivors got up to talk about their recoveries, and it was very personal and a huge event. There were 20,000 people packed into the Boston Garden, and we opened the show with the "Star Spangled Banner." It was practically a religious experience. All the Boston-area bands played, and then Aerosmith closed the show. My wife encouraged me to jump up on stage, and I actually got a chance at the mic with Steven Tyler singing "Come Together."

David is currently performing as the founding member and lead vocalist of Rock Stars & Stripes, a polished, high-impact live rock show with powerful and moving visuals celebrating some of the greatest American rocks artists and hits including music by Boston, Styx, KISS, The Eagles, The Cars, Billy Joel, Lynyrd Skynyrd, Journey, ZZ Top, Night Ranger, and many more. The show takes the audience on a "rock and roll road trip" across the country with a positive, entertaining musical and visual experience. David fronts a seasoned group of All-Star musicians accompanied by an evocative video produced by Emmy and MTV award winning video editor Jeffrey Clark. Rock Stars & Stripes is a patriotic tribute to the people and music of America.

How was Rock Stars & Stripes conceived?

That Boston Strong event was obviously very moving. Seeing the unity and strength from the assembled people of Boston made me start to think about how we are all related to each other. And of course the fact that it was a big rock concert, well it kind of dawned on me: one common bond that many Americans share is their love of rock 'n roll! This is not a show about our political or ideological differences; this is a show about music and our common bonds.

Then it was just a matter of figuring out how to deliver that kind of a show, start to finish, in a compelling way. That led me to presenting the show as a "Rock 'n Roll Road Trip across America" to tie all the great musical areas of the United States together into one show. I wanted the videos to relate directly to the music being performed, so that people got a sense of the areas we were traveling to, the people of those areas, and the music that was created there. We're very gratified that the show is being extremely well-received.

What do you enjoy most about these shows?

No question, the great community vibe and unity that we generate. There's much more to this presentation than just the musical journey! We also have a "Local Heroes" segment, in which we honor individuals for their positive contributions in their communities. We bring them on stage, tell the audience their story, and honor them with a special Rock Stars & Stripes medallion. We also have a Charity of the Evening, which is connected to the local community. It's about paying respect to the communities in which we perform. People leave this show happy, entertained and even a little prouder to be Americans!

Rock Stars & Stripes has a show at the Lesher Center in your hometown of Walnut Creek, how is Tony LaRussa's Animal Rescue Foundation (ARF) involved?

Obviously ARF has been part of the Walnut Creek scene for many years, and now has a national presence as well. I was checking out their website a few months back and hit upon their "Pets for Vets" program, which meshes with our message perfectly; people doing good for their communities. Anyway, we asked them if they would be interested in being our Charity of the Evening for this Lesher show, and we were delighted they said yes! We are donating three wrapped Rock Stars &

Stripes autographed guitars to ARF, one for auction, one for raffle that night, and one which will hang at the ARF HQ. We'll also be selling customized show programs for this event, also to raise money for ARF and "Pets for Vets."

You're a newlywed. Where did you meet your wife, Tamra?

Tamra and I were introduced to each other by our mutual friend, Michael Brandon. We were both happily single, but wow—we just fell head over heels for each other! We were married just this past December 5th in Kona, Hawaii. So yes, we're newlyweds!

In retrospect, I was really happy that I didn't meet her at a show; instead we met in a much more natural way. It's not exactly 'keeping it real' to first set eyes on someone when they're performing on stage. As it turned out, once we were already a couple, the first show she saw me play was Boston Strong! I'm up there on a 75-foot Magnatron screen performing with Boston, in Boston, for the first time the band had played there in 20 years. Then I'm singing with Steven Tyler, and we're meeting all these celebrities backstage. I told her "Honey, not every day is going to be like this!" And she's good with that!

What does the future hold for David Victor?

Of course, we're going to be working hard on booking shows for Rock Stars & Stripes/Rockin' America, as well as my other bands, which includes David Victor "The of Boston and Styx" and David Victor's Super Group, Platinum Rockstars. I'm also enjoying my Strum & Spirits business, which is a music-based team building activity.

Today, David lives a suburban rock star life which includes walking his dogs as well as encouraging his friends and neighbors to come out to his shows. You will be blown away be any of David's shows due to the music, the showmanship and the overall great time had by everyone in the audience. "What's not to love when you know every word of every song," said Christie Killen. David is also busy promoting his Harmony & Healing charity project bringing music to patients and their families in hospitals.

Feel free to add David on Facebook or visit his website at www.davidvictor.com or www.davidvictorpresents.com.

Suzanna Spring
The blending of Music and Yoga

Country singer-songwriter and yoga instructor Suzanna Spring strongly believes that there is a connection between her two passions. "In every element of life there are moments of unpredictability. Music and yoga both are harmonious, combining elements of breathing, movement and focus," Suzanna states. "They are both a dance of grace and strength that unexpectedly brings the mind in tune with the heart," says the charming green-eyed red head I initially met through a mutual friend.

Born in Oak Park, Illinois, Suzanna moved around a lot as the daughter of a commercial pilot. The family eventually settled in Livermore Valley where she graduated from Livermore High School before attending U.C. Davis, studying fine art and design. She began playing the French horn at the age of eight, but it was her mother, a member of a three-piece country band, who taught her to sing and play guitar. "Stylistically, it was my mother who exposed me to the classic country singers." Suzanna's style, in songs and voice, trended more toward the likes of Lucinda Williams, Emmylou Harris and Townes Van Zandt as she played in a series to bands during her college years.

After graduation, her graphic arts career kept her busy and moving around the country; however, performing was still a big part of her life. By 1987, she relocated to Los Angeles to pursue a graduate degree at Cal Arts when an opportunity presented itself to join an all-female band called The Mustangs, a country version of the successful alternative band, The Bangles. During their seven-year run, The Mustangs toured extensively in the western United States, and toured Europe and Scandivavia. Highlights included appearances at the famed Palomino Club, the Los Angeles Country Fest, SXSW (South by Southwest), the Powerhaus in London, the Roskilde Music Festival in Denmark, and the International Country Music Festival in Zurich. Nominated by the California Country Music Association as "Vocal Group of the Year," the Mustangs were featured performers at the Jimmy Dale Gilmore & Friends Show in Austin. Suzanna says there are talks going on currently about a possible Mustangs reunion.

As one of the primary songwriters for the band, Suzanna submitted several songs to a Nashville music magazine as the band was starting to come apart in the mid-1990s. The magazine's editor forwarded the songs to a music producer who encouraged Suzanna to move to Nashville and record with Cary Richard Beare of Riverdogs. Suzanna later secured a publishing deal with EMI as a staff writer before ultimately finding a home at Bluewater Music as a writer and artist. "I loved writing songs, knowing that my job was to let my imagination soar and play music. The time in spent in recording studios was just magic. All of us who lived that lifestyle felt the camaraderie, the mutual appreciation that comes from recognizing a great song when you hear it."

Her first solo album, *She's Got Your Heart*, won Music Row's DISCovery Award and her performances have included Nashville's legendary Bluebird Café, NPR's World & Music Program, Nashville Folk Festival, WPLN's Songwriter Sessions, Nashville's Independent Music Festival, SXSW Music Festival in Austin, and shows in Boston and New York City.

"Suzanna has a beautiful voice, a quick wit and is a gifted songwriter." —Paul Jefferson, Nashville recording artist and acclaimed songwriter.

It was during this period in her life when she also discovered yoga at a Nashville gym frequented by many musicians. "Yoga gave my life balance," says Suzanna. After studying at studios around town she was one day asked to fill in as an instructor, which turned out to be the beginning of a new love and passion. Today, she is a 500-hour certified E-RYT (Experienced Registered

Yoga Teacher).

Following the release of her song, "Time," as a radio single for country recording artist Doug Stone, she returned to California in 2007 to find her hometown of Livermore had become a popular wine region and burgeoning music/film community. She was introduced to vintner/musician Karl Wente who invited her to join in on jam sessions on the front porch of his home. After months of jamming with a host of talented musicians, together they formed *The Front Porch Band*, which played regularly at the summer Home Grown concert series along with a succession of club dates and local gigs. "Playing with a rotating collection of amazing musicians, eventually led me to start my own band, The South Livermore Boys Club band, aka The Surly Jackasses (a name coined by her bandmates)." Suzanna was again a featured artist at SXSW in 2013, invited to play with her band on the Sony City Independent Artists Stage. The band also performed at Craneway Pavilion in 2016 for the Bay Area's largest yoga fundraiser, Yoga Reaches Out, benefiting cancer research and treatment.

Around this same time, Suzanna also began teaching yoga at studios in the East Bay. Three years ago, she and two other yoga instructors, Laurie Johnson Gallagher and Stacy McGinty, teamed-up to open Dragonfly Yoga + Wellness LLC in Downtown Livermore. Suzanna and Stacy have continued as owners, while Laurie remains an active instructor and co-director of the Studios teacher training program. Their highly successful studio resembles a grand ballroom complete with large windows, high ceilings and good acoustics for music. "It has great energy," says the immensely popular instructor.

"When Suzanna teaches there is a magical calmness to the room. Her voice guides me into that peaceful place while her movement inspires fluidity and breathing to create a unique vibration. She cares about every person's comfort and has the skill to make adjustment suggestions without judgment. She is a true gift." —Pam Clemmons.

At present, Suzanna is currently on a hiatus with her band while she writes and performs acoustically. During the holidays, she was the feature act for a holiday showcase at Tommy T's in Pleasanton, performing an amazing acoustic set along with SLBC guitarist Art Thompson. She has also expanded her yoga to include a teacher's collective called the Tonic of Wilderness, the name inspired by a quotation from writer/naturalist Henry David Thoreau. The group offers yoga and nature retreats and has taken students on trips from Calistoga and New England to Costas Rica, Tuscany and Bali. This year she has yoga excursions planned in Yosemite and Spain. "Creating a yoga community has been such a gift. The practice of yoga gives people the tools to face life's ever-changing circumstances," she says.

Suzanna's path is limitless as evidenced by her legions of devoted music and yoga followers.

4 John Floyd Killen
Cover Band King

Much like Elvis, Prince, Madonna, Cher, Beyonce, and Liberace, Floyd's singular name commands the same type of respect and attention from the music world. Loved and admired by fans, critics and his rock peers, Floyd of Floyd's Ordeal, has been off the radar for the last several years. Rumors of a retirement, illness or mental breakdown had all surfaced on conspiracy theory websites. Being the award-winning, investigative journalist I am, it was my goal to track down the reclusive rock n' roll front man who changed my life forever.

It took me months of following every lead imaginable until I found the legendary cover band singer/bass player. I initially heard that he was working as a Mt. Everest Sherpa in Nepal, then a valet car-parking attendant at the Wynn Hotel in Las Vegas and one rumor even had him running with a pack of wolves, somewhere near Yosemite. Much to my surprise he had actually assumed the role of a county manager for a "to remain nameless" title insurance company in San Jose. Candidly, I was disappointed to find Floyd living the M-F/9-5 suburban slow-death existence. For a one-time buttless chaps, dreadlock extension-wearing front man of a classic rock, turned grunge rock, turned alt rock band, who ruled the Bay Area small club circuit from 1993 – 2008, I couldn't imagine a more sad and depressing, cheesy Rotarian profession given the wild lifestyle this rock God lived for roughly fifteen years.

I caught up with the reclusive celebrity while he was trying to pass a kidney stone. It's said a wild honey badger only rests when bitten by a cobra. Similarly, Floyd's cobra is trying to pass a basketball-sized calcium deposit and that had him resting. He may have been in agony throughout our interview, but he certainly was insightful for someone so heavily medicated. When I arrived, he was playing air-trombone and eating animal crackers. After I adjusted his pillows, we spent the next couple of hours catching up and making crank phone calls.

The son of a navy man, Floyd was born in Portsmouth, Virginia, but traveled around a lot until he was discovered and offered a spot as a Disney Kid on the Mickey Mouse Club. Not talented enough to work the states, he was a crowd favorite at the Tokyo Disneyland. Like Justin Timberlake and Nick Lachey before him, he traded in his mouse ears for the acne scars of a boy band. Floyd's Boys, based in Orlando, Florida, did the typical tour of indoor malls until they broke up over the lack of bathroom etiquette on their tour bus. Floyd took this opportunity to get his high school GED and community college AA degree in Fashion Merchandising through a less than reputable online learning center. This is also when Floyd began performing as part of a popular a cappella duo. His partner, Steve Harwell, who later joined the mildly successful and horribly cheesy alt-band, Smash Mouth, left Floyd high and dry when fame called. The popular duo, known as Floyd & Co., played the South Bay coffee house circuit in the mid to late '80s. "I carried Steve's weak singing the best I could with occasional hand clap solos and sang leads whenever he went to the can. Our Tully's world tour was very well received," Floyd says. This senseless break-up did allow Floyd to form the band Floyd's Ordeal; however, open auditions for bandmates lasted almost three years.

There have been many Floyd's Ordeal line-ups over the years, but the one constant has always been Floyd himself. "They tried to replace me at one time, but I controlled 51% of the band's voting power," says Floyd. He doesn't really like to talk why he took this self-imposed sabbatical, but it apparently has something to do with the IRS and unreported income. He's begged me a thousand times to ghostwrite his autobiography, but I'm afraid it would be too emotionally draining on me.

Floyd has been married to his much younger trophy wife Christie for over 26 years. Together they have two beautiful daughters (Karly and Libby). As is the case with many traveling musicians and magicians, it's hard to say how many half-siblings the girls have out there on the road. Floyd struts around the family's cramped two-bedroom condo like he owns the place. They're actually renting. The walls are outfitted with Floyd signed guitars and gold albums. Floyd's Ordeal released several EPs (extended play) albums over the years including *Young Man* (1995), *Chucky's Carp* (1996), *Spinning* (1999), *Interior/Exterior Music* (2002) and the seven-disc FO Greatest Hits/Anthology Box Set (2017). Collectively the band sold a total of twenty-seven units which is just five more than the total number of books I've sold.

Most people think I'm bragging when I tell them Floyd was the best man in my wedding. He wanted to be the flower girl, but my wife said no. Floyd and I became friends at the height of his career while he was living on Easy Street. He actually lived on Easy Street in Mountain View. When I said earlier that Floyd changed my life, he actually did when he gave this wanna-be writer a pen and allowed me to contribute a monthly column to the Floyd's Ordeal fan club newsletter. This early training, dealing with unrealistic deadlines and countless re-writes under a sadistic editor, conditioned me to be the popular columnist I am today. Very few people know, Floyd and I also collaborated on a song entitled "Love 4 Money" from his debut EP. This probably explains why I wanted to name my first-born son, Floyd, but sadly I only had girls. I did pitch the names Floydena, Floyderella or Floydiana, but no luck.

When I asked Floyd about the highs and lows of stardom he gets a little misty eyed when recounting his unhealthy obsession with Mike Peters of The Alarm. "Imagine listening to your favorite band all through college and then years later getting the chance to not only open for them, but become besties with your hero." Floyd's Ordeal opened for The Alarm four times during shows in the Bay Area and Floyd stalked Peters all the way back to Wales where he was asked to perform with him at The Gathering, an annual concert put on by the band for their huge fan base (a couple of dozen equally obsessed Alarm-heads). For those wondering, the low point was playing a nearly empty biker bar for tips and watching his drummer go home with a girl who wasn't necessarily born a girl. No judgment.

Floyd and I have always had a relationship based on mutual respect and out of control good natured ribbing. He's the musician I always wanted to be and I'm the writer he never wanted to be. We have a lot more in common than most people think, but because of our busy schedules it's difficult to find time to just hang out. He is still performing, mostly with his youngest daughter, as an acoustic duo playing at churches, farmers markets and house shows. Floyd may look like an emaciated French performance artist, but he is actually an active ice hockey player and surfer. He also dabbles in photography, home renovations and car repair. He is truly a man of many skills and boundless energy. I hope one day everyone reading this article will get a chance to meet the man, the myth, the legend who is Floyd.

5 The Music in Me

I don't have a musical bone in my body, but I have always loved music. As a kid growing up in the 1960s and 70s, I would listen to Elvis records on my portable record player, playing air guitar and lip-syncing before it was called air guitar and lip-syncing. When I was a little older, I longed to be a member of the Partridge Family or an Osmond Brother. As a teen, I dreamt, <u>actually dreamt</u>, of starting my own band, cutting records and touring the world. My fictitious band name was *Gigolo* and I even designed the t-shirts we would sell at our concerts. They were bitchen'.

Sadly, or some might say unfairly, I can't play any instrument, I can't sing, and despite having a little bit of rhythm, I can't even really dance. I've taken guitar, drum, bass, saxophone and tambourine lessons and can't play a note. Some days I have trouble just playing the radio. Maybe, this hard to admit truth is why I've always been so drawn to musicians. Not drawn in a sexual way, although certain members of the Go-Gos and Bangles were pretty hot in their day and don't even get me started on Nancy Wilson of Heart.

Mike once joined a no-cut a cappella group and they asked him to sing solo. So low no one could hear him. Mitzi Copeland, Mike's sister

Due in large part to my lack of talent, I've been inspired to assist my musician friends by promoting their talents through some of my magical resources. In the early 1990s, I started a booking agency and helped line up gigs for the likes of Floyd's Ordeal, Blue House, The Del Toros, Paul Blote, The Marina Towers Band, Gary Tackett and a little known country artist named

Paul Jaqua (later to be known as Paul Jefferson). Since that time, I've gone on to organize and promote club shows (Suburban Slow Death, Replica, Tyler Stimpson) and produce music fundraisers (MdK, Jeff Campbell, Courtney Randall, Pine & Battery, Static & Surrender and Heather Combs). I've also written numerous profiles on artists the likes of Michelle Maeso, John Floyd Killen, Paul Jefferson, David Victor, Steve Albin and Suzanna Spring. It's not much, but if I was a roof-raising rocker or cerebral coffee house singer/songwriter, I would truly appreciate it if someone would help me generate some much-needed attention for my mad musical skills by penning a feature article on me or inviting me to play a show.

I don't know that I've ever met anyone with less musical ability than Mike Copeland. John Floyd Killen, Founding Member of Floyd's Ordeal

I am a fan of every musical genre, however despite meeting Verdine White of Earth, Wind and Fire at the Viper Room in West Hollywood, I've had more luck meeting rock musicians that country, R&B or hip-hop artists. Over the years, I've been fortunate to meet a few true blue rock stars such as Eddie Money, Brad Gillis of Night Ranger, Eric Martin of Mr. Big, James Hatfield of Metallica and the late/great Ronnie Montrose. I've even separately met four members of one of my favorite bands, Journey – Steve Perry (Scoma's in Sausalito), Jonathan Cain (Ceasars Casino, Lake Tahoe), Ross Valory (Bank of America, San Ramon) and Neal Schon (Shoreline Amphitheater, Mountain View). I was once in a Las Vegas strip club with Axl Rose and Duff McKagan of Guns & Roses, however they were much too preoccupied for me to say hello. Of those that I actually engaged in a conversation with, most were cordial yet distant. Steve Perry was hands down the nicest and most congenial and even invited me to join him for a short time at his table. I got the impression that he has a lot of free time on his hands.

Many have heard my story that during my sophomore year of college, at California State University Northridge, I lived next door to a fun and charismatic girl named Paula Abdul. She was working as the choreographer for the Laker Girls and had aspirations of staging dance shows in Las Vegas. We hung out a fair amount, never dated, but were good friends for over a year. Several years later, I was listening to a catchy pop song *"Straight Up"* on the radio and just about drove off the road when I heard the artist was none other than Paula Abdul. Upon reading her story in People magazine and being blown away by her physical makeover, I wrote her a couple of letters (±200) congratulating her on her success and wishing her well. Alas, there was never a response. Despite the restraining order, I did catch one of her concerts and enjoyed the show immensely. The boy band, "Color Me Badd" opened for her just in case you were wondering. That's Badd with two d's.

In the summer of 2008, my wife and I made a pilgrimage to the Rock and Roll Hall of Fame in Cleveland, Ohio. We spent close to six hours roaming the halls and I could easily have spent six more just wandering all six levels of the 150,000 square foot cathedral. The highlights on our trip included the U2 3D concert film, the Bruce Springsteen and Pink Floyd exhibits and the numerous displays and concert footage. Recently, I visited the Country Music Hall of Fame in Nashville and thoroughly enjoyed that experience too. There was a fantastic *Songwriter in the Round* event with Pat Alger who wrote countless country songs with or for Garth Brooks, Trisha Yearwood, Lyle Lovett, Dolly Parton and Crystal Gayle. Alger performed many of his biggest hits and fielded questions from the audience, mostly me. To be honest, I enjoyed those two museums more than any Smithsonian in D.C.

I've seen close to 100 concerts and shows at venues that ranged from the Cow Palace to Circle Star Theater to the Winterland Ballroom. I've also been to the Hollywood Palladium, Irvine Meadows Amphitheater and Whiskey-a-Go Go in Southern California. I've seen U2, The Police and attended a Day on the Green all at the Oakland Coliseum and I've enjoyed Pablo Cruise, Marc Cohn and Bobby Kimball of Toto at the intimate 220 seat Firehouse Theater in Pleasanton. I've sat in the first few rows for shows by Bon Jovi, Luther Vandross, Bryan Adams, Journey, Kiss, Ray Charles, Hall and Oats, James Taylor, Foreigner, Def Leppard, Janet Jackson, Train, Maroon Five and Madonna. I've also sat in nose blood seats for shows by AC/DC, Styx, REO Speedwagon, Earth Wind & Fire, ELO, The Commodores, Bruce Springsteen, Elton John, Whitney Houston, Jimmy Buffet, Alabama and Bruno Mars. There were also unforgettable shows by Prince, Rod Stewart, The Eagles, The Jackson 5, Fleetwood Mac and The Jackson Five, The Who and Van Morrison. You should've seen my concert t-shirt collection back in the day.

I, long ago, gave up hope that I would ever hear the words, "see you at band practice" or that I would perform on a stage in front of a live audience. However, thanks to the video game Guitar Hero, and living vicariously through my musician friends, there will always be music in me. *#supportlivemusic*.

6 My Concert History

I don't drink (much) and I don't gamble (much) and I certainly don't smoke (except for my medicinal needs), but if I'm being honest, attending concerts and comedy shows has always been a vice of mine. In the past, I've written about my connection to music without ever chronicling the shows I've attended over the years. So, for those of you who are interested, I hope this will help you recall a few of the shows you may have seen and perhaps ever bring back a few treasured memories from your past.

Rock
Bruce Springsteen and the E Street Band
The Who
U2 (2)
Journey (4)
Tom Petty & the Heartbreakers
AC/DC
Kiss
Cheap Trick
Phil Collins
Styx (2)
REO Speedwagon (2)
Foreigner (3)
ELO
Def Leppard (2)
The Police
Peter Frampton
The Doobie Brothers
Fleetwood Mac
Bon Jovi (2)
The Babys

April Wine (2)
Loverboy (2)
Lenny Kravitz
Shooting Star
Alanis Morissette
Europe
Lindsey Buckingham (2)
Night Ranger
Mr. Big
Eric Martin (3)
Greg Kihn
Eddie Money (5)
Kings of Leon
Daughtry
Bad English
Lenny Kravitz
Foghat

Pop
Elton John (2)
Van Morrison
James Taylor
Gloria Estefan and the Miami Sound Machine
Bryan Adams
Pink
Justin Timberlake
Train (2)
Bruce Hornsby (2)
Matchbox 20 (2)
Rob Thomas (2)
Jimmy Buffett
Kenny G
Madonna

Bryan Adams
Patty Smyth and Scandal
Paula Abdul
Janet Jackson
Boz Scaggs
Kenny Loggins (3)
Counting Crows (2)
David Crosby & Graham Nash
Jonathan Cain (from Journey)
Matt Nathanson (3)
Hootie and the Blowfish
Pablo Cruise
Bobby Kimball (formerly of Toto)
John Waite (3)
Plain White T's
Rick Springfield (2)
Tuck & Patty
Jason Mraz
Jewel
Michael Bolton
John Mayer
Maroon 5
The Fray
Snow Patrol
Hall n' Oats (3)
One Republic
Chicago (2)
Marc Cohn (3)
Huey Lewis & the News
The Hudson Brothers
The Sweet Remains
Craig Chaquico (solo acoustic instrumental)

Country
Alabama
The Judds
Wynonna
Travis Tritt
Marty Stuart
Ricky Skaggs
Hal Ketchum
The Band Perry
Little Texas (2)
Charlie Pride
Emmylou Harris
Wynonna
Mustangs of the West
Montgomery Gentry
Clint Black
Lyle Lovett
Sawyer Brown (2)
Paul Jefferson
Rascal Flatts

R&B
Earth, Wind & Fire
The Commodores
The Jackson 5
Luther Vandross (2)
Gladys Knight
Ray Charles
Freddie Jackson
Prince
Whitney Houston (2)
Anita Baker
Smokey Robinson (2)

Dionne Warwick
The Brothers Johnson
Color Me Badd

Comedians
George Carlin
Gary Shandling
D.L. Hughley
Sam Kinison
Cedric the Entertainer
Drew Carey
Russell Peters
Tommy Davidson
Angela Johnson
Bill Burr
Kevin Pollack
Sinbad

Overall Impressions
First Show: The Hudson Brothers at the San Jose Civic Auditorium, 1973

First Real Concert: Foghat, Eddie Money and No Dice at the Cow Palace, 1978

Favorite Concerts: Journey at the Cow Palace, 1981, Prince - HP Pavilion, 2011, Van Morrison - Nob Hill Masonic 2008, Bon Jovi - MGM Grand, Las Vegas 2000

Biggest Thrill: Finally getting to see Tom Petty & the Heartbreakers at the Greek Theater Berkeley, three weeks before he passed away

Biggest Spectacle: Kiss - The Cow Palace, 1979 or U2 - Oakland Coliseum 2012

Biggest Disappointment: Both Whitney Houston shows at Shoreline Amphitheater

Biggest Missed Opportunity: Day on the Green featuring Aerosmith, Foreigner, Pat Travers, Van Halen, AC/DC - July 23, 1978. At only 15, my mom wouldn't let me go.

Coldest Show: Hootie & the Blowfish at Wente Winery, Livermore, 2008

Warmest Show: Alabama at the Cal State Fairgrounds, Sacramento, 1986 – 101 degrees

Loudest Show: Def Leppard at Shoreline Amphitheater, Mountain View, 1986

Coolest Historic Venue Show: Shooting Star at Winterland, 1982

Coolest Club Show: Marc Cohn at Great American Music Hall 1994

Best Circle Star Memory: The Jackson Five, 1974. Heavyweight Champ George Foreman was in attendance.

Epic Last Show: The Keystone, Palo Alto featuring Eddie Money, Greg Kihn, Night Ranger and Eric Martin, 1987

An Unexpected Great Performance: The Band Perry at Super Bowl City in San Francisco, 2017 and Eddie Money's acoustic show at the Caberet, San Jose 1988

Best Seats: Front row center for Bon Jovi at the MGM Grand, Las Vegas, 2006

Surreal Experience: Watching Luther Vandross do his sound check and talking with him at a taping of Alan Thick's *Into the Night* late night show, 1985

Missed Performance: Maroon 5 opening for John Meyer and Counting Crows at the Concord Pavilion. Traffic and parking sucked.

Outstanding Opening Acts (I had never heard of); Jason Mraz opening for Jewel, Kings of Leon opening for U2 and Matt Nathanson opening for Train

Best Vocal Performance: The Sweet Remains at the Firehouse Theater, Pleasanton, 2016. Incredibly beautiful three-part harmonies.

Best Instrumental Performance: Lindsey Buckingham at the Palace of Fine Arts, 2018 and 2008. He is a guitar virtuoso.

Most Historic Venue, The Grand Old Opry – Nashville, 2017

One Song Concert Show – Jennifer Lopez on the Today Show Plaza, NYC 2016

Sweetest Outdoor Venue; Mountain Winery, Saratoga

Most Unexpected Concert Moment: A fight broke out at a Jewel Concert MW 2002

Funniest Comedian: George Carlin at the Circle Star Theater 1978

Filthiest Comedy Show: Sam Kinison, Flint Center, Cupertino 1986

Coolest Rock Star Meeting: Steve Perry of Journey at Scoma's in Sausalito 1993 or James Hatfield of Metallica at Disney On Ice at the Oakland Coliseum 2003

The Lasting Appeal of Boybands
and my lifelong fascination with the genre

As creepy as that headline sounds, please allow me to clarify and expand on the notion that boy bands are now and have always been cool. A boy band (or boyband) is loosely defined as a vocal group consisting of young male singers, usually in their teenage years or in their early twenties at the time of formation, singing love songs marketed towards young women. They often also incorporate choreographed dance routines to perform along with their songs. I'm certainly not saying that I have boyband music on my Spotify playlist . . . OK, if I'm being completely honest there may be a few Backstreet or New Kids songs there, but this music/entertainment phenomenon has shown lasting endurance and I unabashedly admit, it is a genre that has held my attention for almost fifty years.

My boyband admiration, adoration and aspirations probably started with The Osmond Brothers and Jackson 5. As an elementary and junior high school student, with no real academic proclivity, I remember watching American Bandstand and Soul Train, not to mention a host of evening variety shows (Sonny & Cher, Flip Wilson, Tony Orlando & Dawn, etc.), and thinking it would be so cool to be singing and dancing my way through life. As a member of a boyband, I would travel the world applying my craft, while making huge amounts of money and attracting the "lose your mind" attention of the fourteen-to-eighteen-year-old female demographic. Sweet! I begged my parents to birth or adopt four more boys just so I could create my own family boyband in the carport of our suburban home. Two Car Garage Boys was just a working name. Their irritation with my fixation undoubtedly reached a boiling point when their talentless son sang and danced his way through little league baseball games, the school spelling bee and Cub Scouts. It sounds worse than it was, but darn it, I had a dream.

While Motown legends such as the Temptations, Smokey Robinson & The Miracles, The Four Tops, The Isley Brothers and The Spinners might have been on the older side of official boyband status, they did provide the harmonies and dance moves to make a compelling argument that they could be included in the boyband conversation. Don't let me forget Frankie Valli and The Four Seasons, who while they did originally play instruments, this New York based quartet could get down with the best of them. Most of the guys in these 60's and 70's groups grew up together and honed their vocal stylings around a street lamp or in church. These pioneering groups proved to have the right assemblage of talent, looks, sweet dance moves and a swooning female fan base to inspire a rebirth in the genre and the formation of later boybands.

Today's biggest music sensation is BTS, also known as "Bandtan Boys," a seven-member boyband from South Korea. They recently appeared on *Saturday Night Live* and Lorne Michaels was quoted as saying that this was the most popular music act *SNL* had had in the last twenty years. When you think of boybands, you instinctively go right away to *NSYNC, Backstreet Boys, New Kids on the Block, One Direction, 98 Degrees, New Edition (which spawned Bel Biv Devoe), Boys II Men and Nickelodeon's Big Time Rush. Every member of every group has probably made millions of dollars and yet many still perform and tour even though most of the members are now men in their forties. Needless to say, I use the term "boyband" very loosely. The only time a boyband ever breaks up is when a member becomes so popular they don't need to split up the pot anymore . . . Justin Timberlake. Some get hot for a while, like Bobby Brown and Nick Lachey, but they always come back when that popularity fades. Others, like One Direction, who it should be pointed out never took up the choreographed dance moves, are currently on a long hiatus without actually saying they broke up. I give it another twelve to eighteen months before their reunion tour. On the other hand, *NSYNC will probably never get back together given the global musical/acting and *SNL*-hosting appeal of the previously mentioned JT, Justin Timberlake.

An Orlando, Florida-based (PT Barnum type) promotor named Lou Perlman was the opportunistic mastermind behind the meteoritic boyband popularity of The Backstreet Boys,*NSYNC and O-Town. Perlman, who it was later determined made his money operating a long running investment Ponzi scheme that would later send him to prison, was fascinated by the success of New Kids on the Block. Around 1993, with little more than a $3 million initial investment, Perlman ran an open audition/talent show to recruit five teenagers who ultimately became the Backstreet Boys who went on to sell over 130 million albums. Several years later, Perlman struck gold again with the formation of *NSYNC, who sold over 70 million records. Perlman even co-wrote a bestselling book, *Bands, Brands and Billions* before his legal troubles began. Among an assortment of misdeeds, Perlman was sued by virtually every band he discovered and managed for misappropriation of funds and other related offenses. Would you believe, contractually, he was a sixth member of both BSB and *NSYNC collecting royalties in addition to management and agent commissions? Sadly, or not, he died in prison at the age of sixty-two.

With all due respect to the guys, there have been a fair share of pretty terrific girl bands over the years, too, including Destiny's Child (featuring the young Queen B), TLC, En Vogue, The Spice Girls, The Pussycat Dolls and Fifth Harmony to name just a few. Even before those groups came into popularity there was The Pointer Sisters, Sister Sledge and Wilson Phillips. I give it up to these fiercely talented women, but other than that one confusing year in high school, I never dreamed of being in a girl band. Historical recognition should also be made to the girl groups of the 60's included The Supremes, The Shirelles, the Shangri-Las, The Marvelettes and The Ronettes. I guess you could also include The Lennon Sisters, who found fame on *The Lawrence Welk Show*. Just to answer the question, no, I did now watch *LW*, but my dad liked the show.

Despite giving up a lot of their childhoods in exchange for fame and fortune, you don't hear of too many former boyband members going off the deep end and ruining their lives through drugs, crime or college admission cheating scandals. Oh sure, Joey Fatone of *NSYNC was dressed as a rabbit on the reality show, *The Masked Singer*, but it wasn't as bad as it sounds. Drew Lachey from 98 Degrees won season two of *Dancing with the Stars* while his brother, Nick, hosted several music-related reality shows. BSB, Kevin Richardson (Chicago), *NSYNCer Joey Fatone (*Little Shop of Horrors* and *Rent*) and NKOTB member Joey McIntyre (*The Fantasticks*) have all appeared in Broadway musicals. As far as the silver screen, Michael Jackson appeared as the Scarecrow in *The Wiz*, a 1978 musical adaption of *The Wizard of Oz*. More recently, Justin Timberlake of *NSYNC had shown his acting chops in numerous flicks including *Alpha Dog, Trouble with the Curve* and *The Social Network*. Ralph Tresvant of New Edition played Sam Cooke in the biopic *Get On Up*. Donnie Wahlberg of NKOTB appeared in *The Sixth Sense* and is a regular cast member in the CBS series *Blue Bloods*. Just last year, Harry Styles of One Direction was in the World War II epic *Dunkirk*. Kudos to the casting directors who saw the ability to capitalize on the popularity of these multi-talented heartthrobs. Acting was not even a consideration in my boyband pursuits. Perhaps it should have been.

There seems to be a resurgence in popularity in the '80s boybands and many of these acts will be touring this summer. Both New Kids on the Block and Backstreet Boys have both had extended residencies at major venues in Las Vegas. While my dreams of achieving boyband status were never recognized, I always appreciated the talent, hard work and dedication that went into these groups long running successes. I wish these men continued health, happiness and prosperity even if it does come across a little creepy. Don't judge me.

You can't tell the players without a program.

BTS – V, J-hope, RM, Jin, Jimin, Jungkook and Suga
New Kids On The Block – Donnie, Joey, Danny, Jordan and Jonathan
Backstreet Boys – Nick, AJ, Kevin, Brian and Howie
NSYNC – Justin, JT, Lance, Joey and Chris
New Edition – Bobby, Ricky, Ralph, Ronnie and Michael
Bel Biv Devoe – Ricky, Michael and Ronnie
O-Town – Erik-Michael, Trevor, Jacob and Dan
Boys to Men – Nathan, Shawn, Wanya and Michael
98 Degrees – Nick, Drew, Justin and Jeff
One Direction - Harry, Louie, Zayn, Liam and Niall
Big Tim Rush – Kendall, James, Logan and Carlos
Osmond Brothers – Donnie, Alan, Wayne, Merrill and Jay
Jackson 5 – Michael, Jackie, Jermaine, Tito and Marlon

ABOOKS

ALIVE Book Publishing and ALIVE Publishing Group
are imprints of Advanced Publishing LLC,
3200 A Danville Blvd., Suite 204, Alamo, California 94507

Telephone: 925.837.7303
alivebookpublishing.com

www.ingramcontent.com/pod-product-compliance
Lightning Source LLC
Chambersburg PA
CBHW020326170426
43200CB00006B/286